D0928259

STUDENT UNIT GUIDE

NEW EDITION

Edexcel A2 Government & Politics

**Unit 3C Updated
Representative Processes in the USA**

Tremaine Baker

Series Editor: Eric Magee

PHILIP ALLAN FOR
HODDER
EDUCATION
AN HACHETTE UK COMPANY

Philip Allan, an imprint of Hodder Education, an Hachette UK company, Market Place, Deddington, Oxfordshire OX15 0SE

Orders
Bookpoint Ltd, 130 Milton Park, Abingdon, Oxfordshire OX14 4SB
tel: 01235 827827
fax: 01235 400401
e-mail: education@bookpoint.co.uk
Lines are open 9.00 a.m.–5.00 p.m., Monday to Saturday, with a 24-hour message answering service. You can also order through the Philip Allan Updates website: www.philipallan.co.uk

© Tremaine Baker 2014

ISBN 978-1-4718-0463-2

First printed 2014
Impression number 5 4 3 2 1
Year 2018 2017 2016 2015 2014

All rights reserved; no part of this publication may be reproduced, stored in a retrieval system, or transmitted, in any other form or by any means, electronic, mechanical, photocopying, recording or otherwise without either the prior written permission of Philip Allan or a licence permitting restricted copying in the United Kingdom issued by the Copyright Licensing Agency Ltd, Saffron House, 6–10 Kirby Street, London EC1N 8TS.

Cover photo: Fotolia

Typeset by Integra Software Services Pvt. Ltd, Pondicherry, India

Printed in Dubai

Hachette UK's policy is to use papers that are natural, renewable and recyclable products and made from wood grown in sustainable forests. The logging and manufacturing processes are expected to conform to the environmental regulations of the country of origin.

Contents

Content Guidance

Electoral system ● How are presidential nominations secured? ● How is the president elected?
● Congressional elections ● Direct democracy ● Concerns about the US electoral system

Historical context ● Recent ideological partisanship ● Party factions and bipartisanship
● Party decline or party renewal? ● Party support ● Minor parties

Range of pressure groups ● Methods and strategies ● Influence on the federal government
● Power of pressure groups

History of inequality ● Continuing inequalities ● Post-racial America ● Affirmative action
● Immigration ● Latino political significance

Questions & Answers

Getting the most from this book

Examiner tips

Advice from the examiner on key points in the text to help you learn and recall unit content, avoid pitfalls, and polish your exam technique in order to boost your grade.

Knowledge check

Rapid-fire questions throughout the Content Guidance section to check your understanding.

Knowledge check answers

1 Turn to the back of the book for the Knowledge check answers.

Knowledge summary

Summaries

● Each core topic is rounded off by a bullet-list summary for quick-check reference of what you need to know.

Questions & Answers

Exam-style questions

Examiner comments on the questions
Tips on what you need to do to gain full marks, indicated by the icon **e**.

Sample student answers
Practise the questions, then look at the student answers that follow each set of questions.

Examiner commentary on sample student answers
Find out how many marks each answer would be awarded in the exam and then read the examiner comments (preceded by the icon **e**) following each student answer. Annotations that link back to points made in the student answers show exactly how and where marks are gained or lost.

About this book

This guide is designed to help you revise for Unit 3C Representative Processes in the USA for the Edexcel Advanced (A2) GCE in Government and Politics. This unit looks at the electoral and representative processes of America and considers the extent to which they fulfil the role of popular participation and democracy.

The specification

The four topic areas of Unit 3C are set out below:

Topic	Key coverage
Elections and voting	• Knowledge of the electoral processes used in the USA • Evaluating concerns that elections do not effectively hold those in power to account • Awareness of factors which explain the outcomes of recent elections
Political parties	• Knowledge of the ideologies and traditions of the main parties • Awareness of patterns of support for each party • Evaluation of the changing significance of parties • Exploring the role of minor parties
Pressure groups	• Knowledge of different types of pressure groups and how they access the political system • Exploring how effectively groups are able to influence the political process • Evaluating concerns that pressure groups have a negative impact on the US political system
Racial and ethnic politics	• Knowledge of the extent of, and policies to reduce, racial divisions • Evaluation of the extent of racial and ethnic diversity in the USA, including levels of representation and political activism • Key issues in contemporary minority politics

About this guide

The **Content Guidance section** summarises the essential information of Unit 3C including a range of contemporary examples, which are vital to ensure your answers are fully developed and supported. It also includes a range of key terms and a series of examiner tips to help channel your revision into the right areas, plus knowledge checks, which invite you to test various key aspects of your knowledge. These checks are numbered and, at the end of the guide, you can find suggested answers. You can then see how well you did in recalling the key information.

The **Questions & Answers section** includes an array of sample short-answer and essay questions, across all four topics, which are designed to show a range of ability levels. Each answer is followed by a detailed examiner's response which points out what students have done well and also ways in which answers could be improved. You are advised to attempt questions yourself and use this guide to reflect on how you can improve your own responses to potential exam questions.

Content Guidance

Elections and voting

At the heart of the American political system is the fundamental fear of tyranny. In this context elections are seen as a crucial way of preventing any group of people, or individual, from becoming politically dominant and using their power oppressively. Thus the overarching feature of this topic is concerned with an evaluation of *how far the political system fulfils its role of holding politicians to account*. There is considerable debate among political commentators about the extent to which the USA is a truly democratic state and how far the frequency, extent and nature of US elections act as a check on power. While many conservatives are quick to point out the relative openness of the system and the range of opportunities for scrutinising and holding politicians to account, more liberal commentators will point to the growth of what they see as a system dominated in particular by money. For these individuals the system is deeply elitist, whereby the wealthy are able to dominate at the expense of the poor, creating a situation in which a growing number of Americans are apathetic, with many choosing not to participate in the political process or even vote.

Because of these concerns the topic also considers arguments about *the extent to which key aspects of the US electoral system are effective and democratic*, as well as *the debate which surrounds possible calls for reform of these elements of the US political system*. In particular, these include debates over:

- the presidential candidate nominating system
- the role of the Electoral College
- the role of campaign finance
- the lack of congressional term limits
- gerrymandering
- low turnout and participation

Fundamental to an understanding of these debates is an understanding of *how the system works*. Students will therefore also be expected to have an understanding of *the key electoral mechanisms in place in the USA*, both in theory and in reality. This topic will guide you through the various stages of the electoral process for the different branches of government.

A final aspect of the topic is an analysis of *the factors which shaped and affected the outcome of the most recent elections*, whether presidential, congressional or midterm, and their significance.

Electoral system

The US electoral system reflects the federalist nature of the USA, in which power is held by both state and federal governments. The Founding Fathers, in order to ensure

Elitist A description of the idea that political power is held by a small group, or elite. In this book it refers to the idea that certain pressure groups and individuals dominate the political process, due to their wealth or status.

Examiner tip
Specific questions on the outcome of elections will relate to the type of federal election most recently held, either congressional, midterm or presidential. However, more generic questions might refer to the significance of midterms for example, which requires a wider scope of analysis.

politicians are effectively held to account, created a system in which federal elections are both frequent and fixed, with elections taking place every 2 years. In all these elections a first-past-the-post electoral system is used, whereby a simple majority of votes is required for victory.

Knowledge check 1

What is a federal system of government?

Table 1 Overview of the US electoral system

	Term	Total number	Mechanisms
Legislature: House of Representatives	**2-year** No limit on number of terms	435 Single-seat districts	• Seats allocated to each state based on the size of the population • Reapportionment of seats undertaken following a census every 10 years • First-past-the-post in all districts
Legislature: Senate	**6-year** No limit on number of terms	100 State-wide Senate seats	• Every state has two senators • Staggered elections, with one-third being elected every 2 years
Executive: President and vice-president	**4-year** Two-term limit	2 Elected together on the same ticket	• Indirect election via 538 Electoral College votes • Each state (plus Washington DC) is allocated votes based on population • First-past-the-post winner of a state (except Maine and Nebraska) takes all votes, with 270 votes required to win

House of Representatives

The House term is fixed at 2 years due to its exclusive constitutional powers to initiate money bills, which could open representatives up to corruption. The intention was to create a chamber which is closely aligned to current public opinion, with smaller districts within each state, and which could be tightly scrutinised and regularly held to account for its actions. The numbers of districts in each state are regularly reapportioned, to account for population shifts, and in most states redistricting takes place on a regular basis by the state legislature.

Redistricting The process of redrawing the boundaries of electoral districts to account for population changes within a state. In 36 states this is primarily undertaken by the state legislature.

Senate

The structure of the Senate, in which each state receives two senators regardless of size, is designed to uphold the federalist principles upon which the constitution is based, by protecting the interests of smaller states. In addition to this, the 6-year term and the staggered and state-wide nature of US elections are designed to make the Senate a more contemplative body, cushioned from the vagaries of public opinion.

President

The presidential election is designed to provide a compromise in which the executive office embodies the national will of the USA, while also ensuring that the federalist nature of America and the interests of smaller states are upheld. Thus the president and vice-president are elected together on a single ticket under the Electoral College system. This system indirectly elects the presidential ticket across each of the 50 states, plus Washington DC. Each state is allocated a number of votes in the Electoral College, which is equivalent to the number of seats it has in Congress. Voters in each state do not therefore vote directly for the presidential ticket, but for 'electors' who will choose the president and vice-president in the Electoral College.

The size of the Electoral College is equal to the total membership of Congress (435 representatives and 100 senators) plus the three electors allocated to Washington DC, totalling 538 electors. Therefore, to win the presidency, a candidate must take states worth 270 electoral votes.

Most states, with the exception of Maine and Nebraska, apportion all electors on a first-past-the-post, winner-takes-all system. In this way Barack Obama won all 29 of Florida's Electoral College votes in 2012 despite winning by a margin of only 0.8% of the popular vote. The federalist nature of the USA is protected by the fact that all states, regardless of size, have at least three Electoral College votes. Thus small states like Delaware and Wyoming had three electors each in 2012, meaning they were significantly over-represented in comparison to more populous states like California, which received 55 electors.

Knowledge check 2

What is the first-past-the-post system?

The presidential election day is therefore a series of 51 separate contests in which candidates attempt to win a series of state-based elections in order to secure the magical 270 electors needed to secure victory.

How are presidential nominations secured?

Due to the fact that the US voter decides who represents the party in the elections, the process to secure the presidency is a long affair. It can, however, be broken down into a number of stages, each of which needs to be successfully negotiated in order for a candidate to become the president of the USA:

- Invisible primary
- Primaries and caucuses
- National conventions
- Presidential debate
- Election day

Invisible primary

This is the stage which runs up to the first formal primary in the USA, effectively beginning as soon as the last election has ended. It is the period when party candidates position themselves to run for the presidency before the formal series of primaries and caucuses starts. During this time the aims of candidates are threefold — to gain media coverage, to gather endorsements and to secure funding.

Media coverage

Candidates will look to achieve widespread name recognition, attempting to gather media airtime and coverage in the printed press. In particular, they will endeavour to present themselves to potential voters as credible presidential candidates and cover any potential weaknesses in their political CV. Thus, following his withdrawal from the 2008 Republican field, Mitt Romney began positioning himself to run as a conservative candidate in 2012, with speeches at the Lincoln Day dinners, the establishment of his 'Free and Strong America PAC' and fundraising activities for SBA-List (a pressure group committed to electing anti-abortion women to political posts).

Endorsements

After formal announcements that they are entering the presidential race, candidates will also look to gather support from key individuals within the party. Thus, in the race for the Republican nomination in 2012 Romney had secured the support of 41 of the 153 unbound superdelegates by March 2012, something the *National Journal* referred to as his 'path to victory'.

Candidates will also look to gather endorsements from influential groups outside the party who will provide important grassroots support in mobilising a candidate's campaign. For example, 7 months before the first 2012 primary, Michele Bachmann joined almost every other major Republican presidential candidate in speaking at the Faith and Freedom Conference in Washington.

Finance

Perhaps the most important function of this phase is to build up a big enough 'war chest' to fight the long presidential campaign. This is best shown by the early withdrawal of former Louisiana governor Buddy Roemer who, after establishing an exploratory committee to run for the Republican nomination in March 2011, was forced to pull out of the 2012 race in February 2012, having raised only $340,000. In particular, candidates will look to court key pressure groups and political action committees (PACs) which will provide them with valuable funding. Even those candidates looking to secure federal funding understand the necessity to raise sufficient funds early enough to be able to stay in the race. Although candidates can self-finance their campaigns (as Jon Huntsman did in 2012, lending his own campaign $5.1 million), it is enormously costly, and very few candidates have the personal assets to do this.

Primaries and caucuses

The first official stage of the presidential election process is the **nomination stage**, which usually takes place between January and June of election year. The key element in this process is the **primary elections**, in which party supporters in each state vote for delegates to go forward to the party convention, which meets to formally select the party's presidential candidate. Each state is awarded party delegates according to the size of the state population.

Candidates who win a state primary or caucus are allocated a certain number, or all, of those state delegates, who are then pledged to vote for that candidate at the national convention. This number depends on whether states allocate their delegates on a proportional or first-past-the-post basis. Thus in Florida in 2008 McCain picked up all 57 of the Republican pledged delegates, despite only beating Mitt Romney by 5%, while in the Democratic race delegates were split, with Clinton picking up 52 and Obama 39.

Superdelegate Key party members, such as governors or mayors, who are sent to the National Party Convention in order to select the party presidential candidate. They are not, unlike other delegates, pledged to vote for a specific candidate.

Federal funding Money supplied to candidates from the public. In the USA, federal 'matching funds' for the primaries match donations made by individual contributors dollar-for-dollar up to a maximum of $250. Major party candidates may also be eligible to receive a federal grant to help fight the general election.

Table 2 Overview of the key primary and caucus events in the nomination stage

Key date/event	Why important?
Iowa caucus	• Traditionally the first result of the process • Widespread news coverage • Seen as an early indication of which candidates might win • Can act as a springboard for candidates
New Hampshire primary	• Traditionally the first primary result • Widespread news coverage • First major testing ground for candidates • High rate of early dropouts
Super Tuesday (the day on which the greatest number of states hold their primaries)	• More delegates can be won on Super Tuesday than on any other single day • Can 'make or break' candidates • In 2008, it was nicknamed Tsunami Tuesday as so many primaries were held

Examiner tip
The system for electing a party's presidential candidate is very similar to the Electoral College vote. Be careful not to confuse the two. A number of students lose marks each year from a misreading of the question on this area of the topic.

Individual states decide the nature of primaries or caucuses; although there are differences between them, they can roughly be divided into three types. These are compared in more detail in Table 3.

- **Open primaries:** Any registered voter can participate in either the Republican or the Democratic primary, but not both, regardless of the voter's party affiliation. The open primary system is adopted for either party in 17 states, including Georgia.
- **Closed primaries:** Only voters who have declared an affiliation to a party can participate in that party's primary. The closed primary system is adopted for either party by 27 states, including Delaware and Kentucky.
- **Caucuses:** These are a state-based series of meetings between key party members and supporters, in order to select a party's candidate for the presidency, the most notable of which is the Iowa caucus.

Table 3 Summary of the advantages and disadvantages of the different systems in the nomination stage

Nomination system	Advantages	Disadvantages
Open primary	• Increases participation, including independent voters • Encourages politicians to have a wider appeal • Usually more moderate voters, filtering out extreme candidates • Good preparation for election	• Can favour candidates with money and a high media profile • 'Raiding' can occur to choose the opposition's weakest candidate • Voters may be ill informed
Closed primary	• Candidates chosen by loyal electorate • Favours candidates with strong grassroots support in the party	• Harder for party outsiders • Lower participation
Caucus	• Favours the well-organised candidate backed by the party • Greater political awareness of electorate	• Low participation and turnout • Candidates may lack wider appeal

Advantages of the nomination process

Democratic

The system is open to the public and actively encourages a much wider voter participation in the selection of candidates. Indeed the increasing use of primaries was a direct result of the McGovern–Fraser reforms, which followed the victory of Hubert Humphrey, who secured the Democratic nomination in 1968 despite standing in no primaries.

The process is also open to any aspiring candidate. In this way, little-known outsider candidates (insurgents), such as Barack Obama in 2008, can rapidly rise to prominence and secure a party's nomination.

Electoral preparation

The primaries are often used as a testing ground for candidates to iron out political campaigns, establish a network of grassroots support and gauge the demands of the electorate. The gruelling nature of the process also narrows the field and eliminates candidates who do not have the political stamina to secure the presidency. In this way Herman Cain, an early Republican favourite in 2012 with his 9-9-9 tax plan and successes in the initial debates, was forced to suspend his campaign following his inability to deal with various allegations of sexual misconduct.

Policy debate

The process allows for rival policies to be discussed and debated, enriching the level of political debate across the country. The 2008 and 2012 primaries saw a series of debates, which pitted the leading candidates from each party against one another.

Disadvantages of the nomination process

Undemocratic aspects

Primaries add a further layer of elections to the process and some argue that the huge number, and frequency, of US elections adds to a growing sense of voter apathy. Indeed turnout at primaries is often below 10%.

Similarly, the primary electorate is unrepresentative of the population, and tends to be older, wealthier and more ideologically partisan, as seen by the relative success of libertarian Republican Ron Paul in both 2008 and 2012.

In addition, the ability of voters to 'raid' opposition primaries is a particular concern in open primaries. This was most recently seen by the efforts of Democrat activists in Michigan to push fellow Democrats into voting for Rick Santorum in the 2012 Republican primary.

Undermines party control

The lack of party control over the selection process can lead to ill-qualified candidates achieving the nomination, due to a lack of peer review. Thus candidates are chosen based on their personal qualities and campaign skills rather than on their presidential qualities. The introduction of superdelegates to counter this was proven ineffectual

> **Examiner tip**
> A possible question is to evaluate how 'effective' or how 'democratic' the nomination process is. Ensure you are aware of the differences in the focus of these questions. The former requires you to focus on how well the process works and if it is successful. The latter requires an evaluation of how open and fair the system is.

Frontloading The phenomenon by which states, in order to claim a greater influence on the nominating process, have moved their primaries forward in the election cycle. This leads to a compression of the primary calendar, with many primaries falling into the first 2 months of the process.

Knowledge check 3

Why are Iowa and New Hampshire important events in the presidential nomination process?

Examiner tip

Questions might ask about the criticisms of the presidential nomination process and possible replacements. Ensure you are able to mention specific reforms which have been suggested to the system, rather than your personal views.

in 2008, when Democrat superdelegates were reluctant to support Clinton and go against Obama, who had secured a majority of pledged delegates.

The primary process is also deeply divisive to parties, with the bitter personal battles and inter-party rivalry necessary to secure the nomination.

Frontloading

The scheduling of primaries has become vital, with a good showing in early primaries considered crucial. Thus the primaries are being compressed (frontloaded) as states compete to be in the early 'make-or-break' rounds. This has two major effects:

- Insufficient time is allowed for debate and reflection, as candidates with a poor early showing soon drop out. This arguably gives too much prominence to the unrepresentative states of Iowa and New Hampshire, as seen by Michele Bachmann's withdrawal from the Republican race the day after she came sixth in the 2012 Iowa caucus.
- Too much importance is attached to raising funds during the invisible primary, which has further lengthened the process by forcing candidates to announce their candidacy earlier. Whereas in 1960 JFK announced his candidacy only 66 days before the first primary, Mitt Romney announced his candidacy on 11 April 2011 — a clear 308 days before the Iowa caucus.

Financing focus

The primary process favours those who have raised the biggest 'war chest' in the invisible primary, giving too much weight to money and image rather than issues. It arguably creates a political system dominated by those groups and individuals who are able to secure the most money for candidates, and causes the reality of daily politics in America to be overtaken by the need to raise funds for the next election.

Alternative nominating systems

Although the earlier reforms to the nomination process, which have seen the increasing use of primaries, have been largely welcome, there still exists a level of debate over the need for further reform of the system to improve the democratic nature of primaries. The pressure group FairVote has established a bipartisan 'Fix the primaries' campaign, which aims to examine a range of reform options. These include the following:

Regional primaries

As early as 1999 the National Association of Secretaries of State proposed a plan, similar to a number of other regional plans, which would divide the country up into four regions, each of which would hold primaries on the same day, with the sequence being rotated for which region went first. Despite this, some critics claim it would not solve the problem of the cost of elections, due to the fact that a quarter of the country would vote in the first regional set of primaries.

National primaries

A 2008 research paper by the South Illinois University outlined alternative plans for nominating presidential candidates which included a National Primary Plan, in which all states would hold a primary on the same day.

Changed scheduling

Other plans have been proposed which would adjust the scheduling of primaries to overcome the problems of frontloading. These include:

- **The American plan:** Small states would begin the primary season, working towards larger states in ten steps, with states chosen at random.
- **The Delaware plan:** Political writer Steven Hill, writing in a 2008 article for *Prospect* magazine, claimed that the current 'system is utterly broken' and instead called for the introduction of a plan which was originally recommended by a Republican National Committee (RNC) commission in 2000. It relied on 'backloading' primaries, with states placed in four groups according to population size. The smallest states would go first and the largest last.

How is the president elected?

Once the nomination has been achieved, the process for election really kicks off with the national conventions.

National party convention

Knowledge check 4

What is the difference between a pledged delegate and a superdelegate?

The traditional role of the national party convention is to formally select the presidential nominee through a vote of pledged delegates and unpledged superdelegates. However, some commentators argue that because of primaries the conventions now merely confirm rather than select the presidential candidate.

Table 4 Roles of the national party convention

Formal roles	Informal roles
Choosing the presidential candidate Formal vote of attending delegates in which the winner must receive an absolute majority of votes	**Restoring party unity** Opportunity to rebuild party unity following the divisive primaries
Choosing the vice-presidential candidate Chosen by the presidential candidate and confirmed by a convention vote	**Enthusing grassroots support** The party faithful are important foot soldiers who need to be galvanised in preparation for the forthcoming election
Deciding the party platform Agreement of the policies that the party's candidate intends to pursue if elected	**Exciting the electorate** Conventions are important media events which engage ordinary voters, creating a crucial 'bounce' in the polls

Significance

In the formal sense it is arguable that the traditional roles of the party convention are insignificant, and serve no real purpose.

- Conventions are nothing more than a 'rubber stamp', especially given that the party candidate is known in advance. In 2012 Romney's nearest competitor withdrew his nomination by April.
- Genuine policy debate, to create a party platform, has been replaced by the need for unity. Conventions rarely discuss controversial or divisive policy issues as this can

Balanced ticket
Choosing a vice-
presidential 'running
mate' which widens the
electoral appeal of the
presidential ticket, or
counters a perceived policy
weakness — for example,
Obama chose Joe Biden,
the former chair of the
Senate Foreign Relations
Committee.

lead to party splits, as with the Republicans in the 1996 convention over abortion. Similarly, the platform is not binding on the president or party members.

- Vice-presidential candidates are now chosen and announced by the presidential candidate in advance of the convention, as with Romney's choice of Paul Ryan more than 2 weeks before the Republican convention in 2012. However, though often apparent well beforehand, conventions remain an opportunity to present a balanced ticket to the electorate.
- Conventions do play a key role, given the inter-party fighting in primaries, of acting to unify the party. The speeches by Hillary Clinton in 2008 and Rick Santorum in 2012 were designed to heal the party wounds, which had arisen during the primaries.
- There remains the important informal role of presenting a united front to the electorate, which acts as a springboard into the forthcoming election. It gives a post-convention 'bounce' prior to the election campaign — as evidenced, for example, by the Republican grassroots revitalisation and 6% jump in poll ratings following the announcement of the fiscal and social conservative Sarah Palin as the vice-presidential candidate.

Presidential debates

The influence of the media in the presidential election campaign is a much debated subject, with claims that the media are more interested in who is winning — termed 'horse-race' coverage — than in the actual issues. However, the televised presidential debate has come to occupy an important place in the electoral calendar.

Significance

- Some argue the presidential debate is more about style than substance, encouraging sound-bite politics, with little genuine debate. Indeed the much proclaimed victory of Romney in the first presidential debate of 2012 was more about his energy levels when compared to the widely reported 'lacklustre' appearance of Obama.
- It is rare for campaigns to turn on the results of presidential debates, although Reagan used the debates well to challenge the incumbent President Carter on his record in 1980, and to address concerns about his age in 1984.
- Presidential debates can be important in encouraging the turnout of the party faithful or turning passive supporters into active voters, as was the case with Kerry in 2004 when Gallup polling showed he closed the 8% gap on President Bush following the debates.
- Viewing figures vary a great deal but there is a generally declining audience. By 2008 this had fallen to around 50 million, although over 73 million tuned into the vice-presidential debate.

What has affected the outcome of recent presidential elections?

Issues

The candidates' policy positions can affect the voting patterns of the electorate and shape the result of the election. With the exception of 2004, which was dominated by the 'war on terror', the most common issue is the state of the economy. Obama was

Examiner tip
Questions on the
presidential debates are
likely to include a need to
review both the role and
significance of them. Make
sure you are able to give
specific examples of where
they have and have not
been significant in recent
years.

keen in 2012 to portray Romney as a rich and unscrupulous politician, who did not care about 47% of Americans, while championing his own economic populist policies, such as those targeting tax increases at the most wealthy Americans while protecting the middle class.

Fundraising

With the increasing cost of campaigns, the ability to secure campaign finances has become a crucial factor in the election. Thus in 2012 a significant number of Super PACs were set up to support either of the two main candidates. Most notable among these was 'Restore our Future', set up by former Romney aides, which spent in excess of $142 million, and 'Priorities USA action', set up by Obama's former White House aide Bill Burton, which spent nearly $67 million.

Campaign strategy

The strength of a campaign is seen as crucial, especially given the Electoral College system (see below) which has created the need for candidates to focus on crucial swing states and voting groups which can affect the outcome. This was shown in 2012 when the Obama campaign team adopted a successful strategy coined 'the optimizer', which looked to use targeted polling in the advertising war against the relatively better-funded Romney camp.

October surprise

Many political commentators refer to the impact of events in the final weeks of the presidential campaign. The financial crisis was arguably a turning point in the 2008 campaign while the effect of Hurricane Sandy, which caused a media blackout for Romney, impacted on the Republican Party's ability to get its message out to voters in the final days of the 2012 campaign.

Electoral College system

The final stage in securing the presidency is the general election day, in which candidates attempt to win a majority of **Electoral College** votes (as explained previously). This system, designed by the Founding Fathers to indirectly elect the president as a safeguard against 'popular passion', has come under renewed criticism by some in recent years, especially since Bush's victory in the Electoral College in 2000 despite losing the popular vote. However, others are quick to advocate its advantages.

Advantages

- **Upholding federalism:** The system protects small state interests, which are over-represented with three electors. Thus candidates must achieve success across all states, as Obama did in 2012 when he won 26 states plus Washington DC.
- **Ensures a strong government:** The system encourages a two-horse race, which usually provides the winner with a secure mandate to govern. Even in the 2000 election, Bush achieved success in 30 states, with 271 Electoral College votes.
- **Ensures widespread support:** Candidates must have depth and breadth of support in order to win. This was shown by Perot's failure to gain sufficient state support in 1992 to win any Electoral College votes. Another example is the limited

Swing state Unlike safe states, which almost always vote for either the Democratic or Republican candidate, swing states have no obvious affiliation. They have therefore become known as battleground states, as their electors can be crucial in achieving the 270 Electoral College votes needed.

national support for the pro-segregationist candidate George Wallace in 1968, which meant he failed to win any Electoral College voters outside the South.

Disadvantages

- **Undemocratic:** Too many elements of the system are said to be antiquated and undemocratic, as shown by Al Gore's loss in 2000 and the existence of faithless electors, who ignore the popular vote in their home state.
- **Over-representation of small states:** The system causes huge disparities in the level of representation between states, meaning larger states are under-represented. Thus if California were represented on an equal scale to Wyoming it would have 205, rather than 55, electors.
- **Swing states dominate:** Although it prevents populous states from dominating the election, the system does give undue influence to swing states. Thus the elections of 2000 and 2004 hinged on the result in Florida and Ohio respectively. Consequently, these states receive a huge amount of campaign finance and candidate footfall.
- **Minor-party failure:** The system disadvantages minor-party candidates, as seen with Perot's failure to win any electors in 1992 despite polling 18.9% of the vote.
- **Voter apathy:** The existence of safe seats can further encourage low turnout. Turnout in the 2012 election was just 50.1% in Republican Texas, while the Democratic stronghold of Hawaii saw the lowest voter turnout of just 44.5%.

Alternative electoral systems

Although fundamental reform would be very difficult, given that it would require a constitutional amendment, many alternatives to the Electoral College system have been proposed. Other than calls for a direct election based on the national popular vote, alternatives include the following:

- **Congressional district method:** This system, which is used in Maine and Nebraska, would allocate electors according to the vote in each congressional district. Thus in Nebraska in 2008 Obama gained one Electoral College vote, even though he lost the overall popular vote in the state; this would not have occurred had Nebraska used a first-past-the-post system.
- **Automatic plan:** This minor reform would automatically allocate state votes, thus preventing the existence of faithless electors.
- **Proportional plan:** This would allocate Electoral College votes in each state proportionally, according to the popular vote. Although this might advantage minor parties, it could make it harder for one candidate to achieve a majority. Furthermore there are fears that it could be used by partisan state officials to win Electoral College votes in states where they cannot achieve a plurality of the vote. This was the case with a 2013 bill, introduced into the Pennsylvania state legislature by its Senate Majority Leader, which would have gained the Republicans a future share of the 20 relatively safe Democrat electoral votes.

Congressional elections

Congressional elections are sometimes dominated by a national agenda, such as with the 1994 Contract with America, or can be overshadowed by the presidential elections.

Faithless elector A member of the Electoral College who does not vote for the winning candidate from their state, who they are pledged to vote for. This was seen in 2000, when Barbara Lett-Simmons, the Washington DC elector, filed a blank vote in protest over lack of congressional representation.

Examiner tip
As well as understanding the different reform proposals, you should also be aware of the strengths and weaknesses of these systems. An easy way to evaluate these is to measure the alternative systems against the advantages and disadvantages of the Electoral College system.

In particular, congressional candidates may benefit from the 'coat-tails effect', where they benefit from the popularity of a presidential candidate. Usually, however, these elections have a more local focus, with many battles taking place over local matters and the issue of pork barrel politics. The result of this is the creation of a system which massively benefits incumbents, with re-election rates rarely falling below 90% for the House, with the Republican surge of 2010 still witnessing an 85% incumbency rate.

Reasons for incumbency advantage

- **Gerrymandering:** The redrawing of political boundaries to gain a political advantage has created a system whereby very few seats are competitive. Political analyst Charlie Cook's political report claims only nine House seats will be in the balance in the 2014 elections.
- **Finance:** Incumbents enjoy a huge funding advantage — in 2012, for example, House incumbents raised on average $1.6 million compared to just $267,000 for challengers.
- **Pork barrelling:** Not only do incumbents have specific name recognition, they are also able to point towards a proven track record in benefiting their constituents. Senator Thad Cochran was labelled the 'king of pork' in 2010, attaching earmarks to 240 projects worth $490 million.

Midterm elections

As most recently seen in 2010 there is a growing phenomenon of midterm elections being dominated by a larger national agenda. Midterms, which take place in the middle of a presidential term, are increasingly being seen as a referendum on the president, with the incumbent president's party losing seats in Congress. However, the significance of these elections has been the subject of some debate:

- **1994 Republican revolution:** The Republicans swept to victory with their Contract with America, gaining 54 seats in the House and eight in the Senate.
- **2002:** The midterm elections were held 14 months after 9/11 and saw unusual gains for Bush's party, which picked up ten seats in total.
- **2006:** On the back of the liberal 100-Hour Plan, the Democrats swept to victory by taking control of both the House and the Senate for the first time since 1994.

In this way, although midterms tend to have a lower turnout and profile than presidential elections, they are significant in shaping the national political climate, by pushing issues onto the national agenda, and also in affecting the remainder of a president's term. This was best shown by the results and effects of the 2010 midterms.

Results and effects of the 2010 midterms

- **Referendum on Obama:** The results reflected discontent over Obama's healthcare and economic stimulus, forcing him to adopt a more compromising tone. However, victory in 2012 gave him a clearer mandate to push for more controversial reforms, such as those dealing with gun control and immigration.
- **Gridlock:** Many Republicans have been emboldened to be more uncompromising and forceful, as seen with the extension of Bush tax cuts in 2010 and most recently the moves towards budget sequestration during the 2013 budget negotiations.
- **Republican resurgence:** The Tea Party agenda of fiscal conservatism and limited government clearly dominated the 2010 midterms, with notable victories including

Pork barrel politics
The idea that congressmen focus on channelling government funds into their home state or district. They are thus judged on their success in gaining federal spending projects for 'the folks back home'.

Earmarks These are attachments to congressional laws, which direct funds to be spent on specific projects, and are a means for congressmen to channel funds to their home state or district.

Examiner tip
There is considerable crossover between topics in this unit, for example with the detail on the Contract with America and the 100-Hour Plan falling into the parties section. If you struggle to retain knowledge, try to focus on examples which can be used across a range of topics and may be useful with different exam questions.

Budget sequestration
This is the far-reaching automatic spending cuts which were set to come into place in January 2013. These mandatory reductions in federal spending were established in the 2011 Budget Control Act a means of cutting the federal deficit.

Marco Rubio in Florida. However, more recently this faction has been forced to compromise its position following Obama's victory and the Republican failure to secure control of the Senate in 2012.

Direct democracy

Direct democracy, in which decisions are made directly by the people rather than by the federal government, is undertaken in many US states. Some states allow for voters to petition legislatures to directly remove elected officials, under **recall** election procedures, and also to veto a state bill, under procedures for calling a **referendum**. However, by far the most common and effective method is the use of propositions, or **initiatives**, as seen by the widespread ballot measures voted on in the 2012 election. These included the issue of same-sex marriage, which resulted in it being effectively legalised in Maine, Maryland and Washington.

Advantages of propositions

- **Controversial subjects** which state legislatures are reluctant to tackle can be voted on, as with the attempted legalisation of marijuana in California Proposition 19.
- They **increase participation** and turnout, as seen with the propositions placed on the ballot in many swing states in 2004 to try and increase the Republican vote, such as the Ohio proposition to ban same-sex marriages.
- Propositions **increase accountability** of politicians, who are forced to be responsive to voter demands, such as Florida's 2008 ban on gay marriage.
- They **engage the electorate**, who become better informed and are encouraged to join pressure groups in response. In 2010, all six Colorado propositions were defeated by the electorate, including attempts to severely restrict abortion.

Disadvantages of propositions

- They can be **inflexible** and undermine the principles of a representative democracy by tying the hands of state legislatures. In this way California Proposition 13, which prevented property tax from being raised, has limited politicians' ability to tackle the spiralling budget deficit.
- They can be **manipulated by wealthy groups**, as seen by the hiring of public relations firm Schubert Flint to run the successful Proposition 8 campaign, which initially banned same-sex marriages in California.
- A **tyranny of the majority** is created by disadvantaging minority groups, for example the effect of California Proposition 209 on African Americans.

Concerns about the US electoral system

There remains considerable debate over the extent to which US elections hold politicians to account. This has led to the passage of a number of reforms which have attempted to restrict funding or make the system fairer.

Proposition A state-based initiative by which voters can force a public vote on an issue by obtaining a petition signed by a certain minimum number of registered voters.

Examiner tip
With this topic, ensure you do not confuse US propositions, which originate from citizens and affect states laws, with UK referendums, which originate from Parliament and affect national laws. It is best to avoid answering proposition questions by adapting AS questions on UK referendums.

Edexcel A2 Government & Politics

Funding

The system of generating campaign finance, which tends to benefit incumbents or wealthy individuals, as well as the increasing cost of electoral campaigns, has led to calls for greater restrictions on campaign finance. The problem has been in securing reform which strikes a balance between creating a fair playing field and not impinging on democratic rights to freedom of expression.

Table 5 Summary of the key campaign finance reforms

Reform	Key terms	Effects
Federal Election Campaign Act 1974 (FECA)	• Limited expenditure of candidates • Provided federal 'matching funds' • Limited the amount individuals and corporations could donate	• *Buckley* v *Valeo* (1976) struck down limits on candidate expenditure, unless they accept public financing • Saw the rise of PACs to circumvent restrictions on donations
FECA amendment 1979	• Allowed parties to raise and spend money	• Rise of **'soft money'** funding, which is money not openly given to a candidate's campaign but which is given to parties which are able to use it to assist a candidate's election
Bipartisan Campaign Reform Act 2002 (BCRA)	• Abolished 'soft money' • Increased individual contribution limit • Restricted non-party advertisements which identify a federal candidate	• Proliferation of 527s, raising money as 'independent' groups • *Citizens United* v *FEC* (2010) overturned advertising restrictions, allowing corporations and unions to promote a candidate. This has seen a rise of Super PACs with unrestricted spending

Despite these reforms, the cost of elections continues to escalate, with the **Centre for Responsive Politics** estimating that over $2.6 billion was spent on the 2012 presidential election.

> **Examiner tip**
> Campaign finance will probably not be the sole subject of essay questions. However, you should understand the reasons for and consequences of campaign finance reforms, which may well be a short-answer question and specifically links to the pressure groups topic.

Congressional term limits

The huge incumbency advantage has led some political commentators, like Lawrence Lessig, to compare Congress to the communist Politburo in terms of length of tenure. Similarly, congressmen are criticised for being so fixated on re-election that they have become overly concerned with developing relations with key donors and pork barrel politics. This has led to calls, from groups such as the Heritage Foundation, for congressional term limits, similar to the presidency (see Table 1, page 7). However, recent attempts by House Republicans to secure a constitutional amendment which would introduce congressional term limits, led by Arizona representative Matt Salmon, has so far gained very little support in Congress.

Gerrymandering

In most states, because the redrawing of political boundaries is undertaken by state legislatures, it has led to widespread claims that the system is open to abuse from

Bipartisan Refers to a political system in which two opposing parties seek to compromise their political positions in order to reach a shared agreement on policy matters. In this way parties govern through cooperation and negotiation rather than opposition and adversity.

unfair partisan gerrymandering. Examples such as the Maryland 3rd district and the Illinois 4th '**earmuff district**', connecting two Latino areas by a thin strip of land, have been criticised as a manipulation of the electoral system. Many states, such as California following the approval of Proposition 20 in 2010, have handed control to a bipartisan redistricting committee. Indeed groups such as FairVote have called for Congress to pass a Redistricting Act, which would require state legislatures to appoint independent commissions.

Participation

Turnout in US elections is one of the lowest of any western democracy, with turnout for the 2010 midterms standing at just over 41%. Reasons for this include:

- **The first-past-the-post system,** along with the use of **gerrymandering**, creates safe seats in which a vote for certain party candidates is wasted. A system in which huge numbers of votes are not counted discourages people from voting.
- **The frequency of elections,** which often take place all year round for various local, state and national posts, can lead to voter apathy. Similarly, the increasing **length of election cycles**, especially with the addition of invisible primaries due to frontloading, can lead to electoral boredom.
- **Registration procedures** are difficult and present a further barrier to voting. Attempts have been made to simplify the process, for example with the 1993 Motor Voter Act, which allowed citizens to register to vote when applying for a driving licence. However, estimates suggest that universal voter registration would increase turnout only by between 8 and 10%.
- **The electorate's perceptions** are important, with some highlighting how the system produces a lack of choice and is controlled by a wealthy elite with little hope for ordinary voters to change the system. Indeed, with turnout being less than 40% among the poorest fifth of the population, there is some weight to this argument.

Advocates for reform of the system thus propose an array of measures to tackle the problem. However, the main suggestion is for the implementation of a more proportional electoral system, such as national popular vote (NPV), followed by instant runoff voting (IRV) or preferential voting.

Knowledge check 5

What are the election cycles for the House of Representatives, Senate and presidency?

Knowledge summary

- Knowledge and understanding of the various electoral processes in place in the USA, including those of primaries, presidential candidate selection, presidential and congressional elections and those which allow direct democracy to take place.
- Ability to critique these processes by evaluating the benefits and drawbacks of each of the mechanisms used in the US electoral system.
- An understanding of the factors which have affected the outcome of recent federal elections, including the most recent election.

- Ability to evaluate the extent to which US elections hold politicians to account, and the reasons for criticisms of the existing system, and possible reforms of it.
- Awareness of the criticisms of, and alternatives to, aspects of the system, including the Electoral College, presidential candidate nomination system, campaign finance, congressional term limits, gerrymandering, and low voter turnout.

Political parties

Unlike their British counterparts, American parties have traditionally been seen as broad, non-ideological coalitions representing a number of regional and sectional interests. Students should be aware of the strong thread of localism and regionalism which runs through the US political system, due to the decentralised nature of the federalist system and the relative independence of state-based party structures.

The first aspect of this topic is therefore concerned with *the extent to which US political parties have become more ideologically cohesive* in their values and policies. While many scholars agree that there is a trend towards a much greater ideological polarisation of the two main parties, in recent years the relative influence of the different factions within each party has been the subject of much debate among political commentators.

This debate has also led some commentators to suggest that there has been an overall resurgence in the importance, and power, of political parties within the US political system. These political commentators point towards the growing centralisation of US parties, as a result of the use of soft money financing and the increasing powers of party leaders to effectively choose congressional committee chairs, as evidence of this rising party power. In contrast, others have argued that the role and functions of political parties have been undermined by other bodies, such as pressure groups, meaning they are in serious long-term decline. They suggest that the powers of US party leaders are constrained by both the candidate-centred, regional nature of the US political system and by their relative inability to influence candidate selection due to the proliferation of party primaries since the 1970s.

A third area to consider is the *impact of these shifts on the traditional support base* of each party. Although it is hard to pinpoint a 'typical' Republican or Democrat voter, there are certain historical and contemporary factors which shape the voting patterns of particular groups. Thus students will be expected to understand which groups tend to vote for each party and the reasons for this support.

The final area in this topic is the nature of the party system itself, and *the factors which have limited the success of minor parties* and given the two main parties such a dominant position in the US political system. Although there are numerous obstacles to minor-party success, especially electorally, there is a requirement for students to engage in a political discussion about the extent of minor-party impact at both a local and national level, and particularly in congressional and presidential elections.

Historical context

For much of America's history the main parties were little more than loose coalitions of individuals serving the interests of a range of groups in society. Although traditionally seen as 'umbrella' parties a number of key events have helped shape the current positions of both the Democratic and Republican parties.

Polarisation The process by which party ideologies and political opinions have become increasingly divided, whereby the views of moderates are overshadowed by the more extreme views and factions in a political party. Thus the rise of the fiscally conservative Tea Party Republicans has arguably shifted the Republican Party further to the right of the political spectrum.

'Umbrella' parties The idea that the decentralised nature of US politics has led to weak party structures in which both main parties encompass a broad range of ideologies and groups within them which are very loosely united under the banner of one party.

New Deal Coalition

Prior to the Great Depression, the support base of the Democratic Party traditionally came from the **Solid South** — white supporters in the southern states who largely rejected the Republican Party due to its role in the civil war and support for the abolition of slavery. It also included recent immigrants, such as those from the Irish and Italian communities, who were mainly based in northern cities.

However, following the establishment of the New Deal by President F. D. Roosevelt in the 1930s, the Democratic Party widened its support base to include a number of new groups. These included blue-collar workers, who benefited massively from the range of government-funded programmes established under the New Deal and the protections it introduced for trade unions; and various minority groups, especially the poorer racial and ethnic minorities, who benefited from the increasing benefits and jobs created by the programme.

Breaking the Solid South

The 1960s saw a realignment of the party positions following the Democratic support for the Civil Rights movement in the 1950s and 1960s, and the exploitation of this by the Republicans. The Democrats in the South, previously regarded as pro-segregationists, saw their dominance eroded by the Republican 'Southern Strategy' adopted by Richard Nixon, which actively targeted the conservative states in the South.

Recent ideological partisanship

These historical events have arguably produced a more polarised party system, in which the Democrats seem to have become the party of the liberal left, while the Republicans have become more clearly that of the conservative right.

A number of commentators point towards the highly partisan nature of US politics today, with many blaming this on the loss of a spirit of compromise which had previously been seen in Washington. Indeed the heated negotiations between the Republicans and Democrats over the 2013 fiscal cliff, which would have seen budget sequestration and wide ranging tax increases, shows this lack of conciliation. Many people point towards the fact that moderate views within the Republican Party have been sidelined, as shown by the fact that Mitt Romney had to move increasingly to the right to secure the party's nomination in 2012, particularly distancing himself from the 'Romneycare' system he introduced while he was governor of Massachusetts. Similarly, the loss of many conservatives from the Democratic Party, whose numbers fell to just 14 members following the 2012 election, shows how the party has become increasingly dominated by those on the left. Indeed one CNN contributor, John Avalon, claimed in 2012 that US politics was 'more polarised than at any point in recent history' with many now claiming that the USA is a politically divided society, in which the Republicans have become a largely right-wing conservative party in stark contrast to the more left-wing liberal Democratic Party.

Examiner tip

With any question about the ideological divisions between the two main parties, make sure that you focus on the *current positions* of the parties with recent examples and evidence. Dated examples, though given some reward, will not show the examiner your ability to fully evaluate and judge the contemporary positions of the two parties.

Partisan An adversarial political system, in which parties compete for power and hold sharply different ideologies. In this system politicians from one party wholeheartedly support their party's policies and are often reluctant to acknowledge the accuracy of their political opponents' views.

Conservative Republicans

Since the Republican resurgence in the 1994 midterm elections, in which the Republicans promoted their Contract with America, the Republican Party has moved more sharply to the right. This nationally agreed manifesto committed party members to vote on a series of conservative issues, such as cutting taxes and balancing the budget. This was further entrenched by the activities of Newt Gingrich, then House Speaker, to enforce a greater degree of party discipline in Congress through the actions of party whip Tom 'The Hammer' DeLay; and with the implementation of the K Street Project, which attempted to increase the number of conservative PACs and lobbyists in Washington. Further evidence of the dominance of conservatives within the Republican Party can be found in the following:

- Despite claims that he was a 'compassionate conservative', during the era of George W. Bush's social conservatism, he restricted access to federally funded abortion services and blocked attempts to introduce stem cell research in the USA.
- There has been opposition to Obama's key policies. For example, almost every single House Republican voted against both the 2009 economic stimulus package and the 2010 Healthcare Act.
- Recent partisan voting in the Republican-dominated House has seen both the passage of the fiscally conservative Paul Ryan Budget, which was supported by all but ten Republicans, and measures to ban abortions after 22 weeks, which gained the support of all but six Republicans.
- There were further primary challenges to moderate Republicans in 2012, such as the Tea Party backed candidates Richard Mourdock, who unseated six-term Republican Senator Dick Lugar in Indiana, and Ted Cruz, who defeated the more moderate David Dewhurst in the Texas Senate primary.
- Hyper-partisanship has been seen in the decision of moderate Republican Olympia Snowe not to stand for re-election in 2012. She claimed her decision was driven by the 'atmosphere of polarisation' which now pervades Congress.
- In 2010 the Republican National Committee ran for office on a conservative 'Pledge to America'. It also required GOP candidates to support a 'purity' resolution, which required them to adhere to a conservative ideological platform, in order to secure party funding.
- In the 113th Congress 93% of House Republicans have signed the Taxpayer Protection Pledge, laid down by the fiscally conservative lobbyist Grover Norquist, which binds them 'to oppose any and all tax increases'.

Liberal Democrats

The Democrats, in contrast, have arguably adopted a more liberal agenda and policy position on many economic and social issues, such as those regarding government intervention and same-sex marriage. Evidence of this shifting position can be seen from the following:

- In 2006 the Democrats wrested control of the House and Senate from the Republicans with a clearly liberal 100-Hour Plan.
- The Democrats have supported a range of bailout, fiscal stimulus, and job creation measures, including: the 2009 economic stimulus plan, which gained the support of all but 11 House Democrats; the $85 billion taxpayer bailout for car manufacturers;

Knowledge check 6

What are midterm elections?

Hyper-partisanship
The idea that the two main US political parties are deeply polarised and in continual conflict. It is seen in the intense disagreements between both Democrats and Republicans, and the adversarial and combative language they use in the media.

100-Hour Plan
The commitment by Democrats to use the first 100 hours of legislative time in Congress to pass a number of liberal measures. These included the establishment of affordable healthcare and the raising of the minimum wage.

Examiner tip

Exam questions will often focus on the extent to which there are ideological differences between the two main parties. You should therefore look to provide evidence for both sides of the argument. Without this balanced examination of the arguments, regarding similarities and differences between the parties, you will fail to pick up many synoptic or evaluative marks.

Examiner tip

Stronger students will be expected to give detailed and specific examples of the various factions and their influence on the policy direction of each party. Simply identifying that a Northern Democrat differs from a Southern Democrat, or that both parties are broad-church organisations with a range of ideologies within them, will get limited credit.

and Obama's 2011 job creation plan, which would have spent $447 billion on stimulating employment in the USA.

- Democrats have consistently called for increased taxes on the most wealthy in order to pay off the national debt. This has been seen by Obama's continual calls for tax rises on individuals earning over $200,000 and his 2014 Budget proposals, which called for Congress to enact legislation in which the rich would pay no less than 30% of their income in taxes.
- In contrast to the Republicans only one representative is a signatory to Grover Norquist's Taxpayer Protection Pledge in the 113th Congress.
- In December 2010 the Democrat-controlled Congress repealed the controversial 'Don't ask, don't tell' policy, which prohibited openly gay persons from serving in the military. In the vote every single Democrat senator voted for the repeal.
- Following recent massacres in Aurora and Newtown the Democratic Party has led the way in trying to introduce gun control measures. This has seen the passage of strict laws through the Democratic-controlled state legislature of Colorado which limit the availability of certain ammunition magazines and require strict background checks on those purchasing fire arms in the state.

Party factions and bipartisanship

Despite considerable evidence of an increasing partisanship, both parties still have a number of core factions which serve to influence and shape the policy directions of the party in some way. Indeed the regional diversity of America, and the increasing use of primaries to select candidates, mean that, despite temporary dominance by ideological groups, the practical considerations of winning elections lead both sides to retain a broader ideological base. This is partly in order to win over the political centre ground, while also appealing to the individual ideological positions of the electorate in the various states and congressional districts across America. As a result, both parties include a range of factions, which compete for influence within the party.

Republican Party factions

There are three main factions within the Republican Party.

Fiscal conservatives

This group advocates free-market economics, a minimalist governmental approach to the economy and a balanced federal budget. Fiscal conservatives specifically promote a programme of reducing both business and personal taxation, moderating the regulation of businesses and cutting government expenditure. The influence of this faction within the party has most recently been evidenced by the rise of the Tea Party Caucus in both the House and the Senate. Indeed the clash of Tea Partiers with old-guard Republicans was best witnessed by their zero tolerance approach to the 2013 budget negotiations, in which John McCain lambasted as 'bizarre', the refusal of leading Tea Party Republicans, such as Ted Cruz and Marco Rubio, to consider raising the US debt ceiling. Leading members of this faction include:

- Republican vice-presidential candidate **Paul Ryan**, who is chairman of the House Budget Committee and architect of the Path to Prosperity Budget plan, which aims to cut spending and balance the federal budget in 10 years.
- Texan Representative **Ron Paul**, the influential Republican with libertarian views, who created a stir during the 2012 presidential nomination.
- Congressional newcomers, brought in on what has been described as the 'Tea Party tidal wave' of 2010, including Kentucky Senator **Rand Paul**, who proposed a bill to cut $500 billion from the federal budget on his first day in the Senate.

Social conservatives

Often referred to as the 'religious right', this faction encompasses a range of Christian political groups which advocate a set of deeply conservative social policies. These include opposition to abortion, same-sex marriage and stem cell research. Indeed the increasing influence of the social conservatives within the party is best evidenced by the comments of former Senator Arlen Spector, following his 2009 defection to the Democratic Party, when he said that the 'Republican Party has moved farther and farther to the right'. Many members of the party have been forced to adopt a more orthodox conservative stance on these issues in a bid to secure the party's nomination for president, most notably Mitt Romney in 2012 and John McCain in 2008. Leading members of this faction include:

- Former Senator **Rick Santorum**, who came second in the delegate count for the 2012 Republican presidential nomination. He stated his support for a constitutional ban on same-sex marriage and made clear that he favoured a complete ban on abortions, even in cases of rape.
- Oklahoma Senator **Tom Coburn** who, according to the *National Journal*, held one of the most conservative voting records of the 112th Congress. In particular he is a strong opponent of abortion, sponsoring a number of bills which limit abortion coverage and those which restrict same-sex marriage, such as the 1996 Defence of Marriage Act, which prevented federal government from recognising same-sex marriage.
- House Speaker **John Boehner**, who claimed the No Taxpayer Funding for Abortion Act, part of the Republican 'Pledge to America', which was passed by the House in May 2011, was one of the 'highest legislative priorities' of the 112th Congress.

Moderates

The Republican moderates tend to adopt a less conservative view towards many aspects of social and fiscal policy. The faction has become known as the Main Street Partnership, because of its more moderate and centrist views. The influence of the moderates, however, previously a dominant force in the party, has arguably declined in recent years. This is perhaps best evidenced by the fact that the last two presidential candidates, despite being seen as previously moderate individuals, were forced to adopt more conservative positions in order to secure the party's nomination. In 2008 McCain's stronger position on immigration, and his choice of Sarah Palin as his vice-presidential candidate, were crucial in galvanising Republican grassroots supporters and key conservative donors to his presidential bid. Similarly, in order to run successfully in 2012, Mitt Romney was forced to abandon his previous commitments

Libertarian The idea that individual liberty is the central factor which any government should look to uphold. It thus involves the belief that individuals should be given the maximum personal and political liberty, while government should minimise its involvement in people's lives.

Knowledge check 7

Name three specific moderate or conservative factions within the Republican Party.

to 'preserve and protect a woman's right to choose' and to defend his Massachusetts healthcare law, labelled 'Romneycare'. The main members of the moderate faction include:

- Maine Senator **Susan Collins**, who has given a degree of support to both legalised abortions and gay rights. She was one of only eight Republican senators to vote in favour of the repeal of the 'Don't ask, don't tell' policy.
- Pennsylvania Representative **Charlie Dent**, who since 2007 has been co-chair of the Republican Tuesday Group, a group of moderates who meet weekly to discuss mutual policy priorities. In the 113th Congress it retained 45 Republican moderate members, a similar number to the House Tea Party Caucus.

Democratic Party factions

Similar to the Republicans, there are three main factions in the Democratic Party:

Liberal activists

6 for '06 agenda
The liberal platform, agreed by Democratic members of Congress, mayors and governors, upon which the 2006 midterms were fought. Under the overarching banner 'A New Direction for America', the Democrats committed themselves to providing real security, better jobs, access to college, energy independence, affordable healthcare and retirement security.

This faction consists of a broad range of members who are committed to a more progressively liberal agenda. This would include defending those rights which are seen to be most threatened by the conservative right: advocating wider healthcare provision, as well as upholding a range of rights for gay people, racial minorities and women, specifically abortion. The rising influence of the liberal activists within the party dates back to the success of the liberal 100-Hour Plan and the 6 for '06 agenda, which saw the Democrats sweep to power in the midterm elections of that year. The Congressional Progressive Caucus currently remains the biggest faction among House Democrats, with 71 members. Prominent Democratic progressives include:

- House Minority Leader **Nancy Pelosi**, who was a founding member of the Congressional Progressive Caucus and key architect of the 6 for '06 agenda. Since then she has been instrumental in the passage of the 2007 Fair Minimum Wage Act, the 2009 Economic Stimulus package and the 2010 Healthcare Act.
- Senator **Sherrod Brown**, who was again judged to be one of the *National Journal*'s 'most-liberal senators' in 2012. He has been a strong advocate of equal rights for gay people, originally voting against the Defence of Marriage Act.
- President **Barack Obama**, who, during his short tenure as a senator, was reported as being the most liberal senator of 2007. Since becoming president, he has made clear his personal support for gay marriage, overseen attempts to introduce comprehensive immigration reform which would provide a 'pathway to citizenship' for illegal immigrants, and has proposed a range of job stimulus programmes.

Moderates

The roots of this modern-day faction lie in Democratic attempts to win back the White House under Bill Clinton, and in the establishment of the centrist Democratic Leadership Council. In this way the moderates adopted a more pragmatic approach to policy development, which attempted to appeal to both the conservative heartland of America and the more progressive elements of society. In its current form the most prominent congressional group is the New Democrat Coalition (NDC), which stated that it was the 'largest coalition of moderates heading into the 113th Congress', with 51 Members. Though the moderates appeared to lose influence following Al Gore's loss in the 2000 presidential election and the subsequent rise of progressives within the party, they still have a moderating influence on the party, especially since the loss of the House in the 2010 midterms and the subsequent need for greater compromise and bipartisanship. Key figures include:

- Former Secretary of State **Hillary Clinton**, a former member of the Senate NDC, who seems to be positioning herself for a run at the party's candidacy for president in 2016.
- Chairman of the NDC **Ron Kind**, who has pushed for legislation which would end the $292 billion of farm subsidies paid out from 1995 to 2010, while also supporting moves towards bipartisan immigration reform.
- Colorado Representative **Jared Polis**, who is the co-chair of the LGBT Caucus, and one of the few openly gay members of Congress. He is also a leading member of the NDC, advocating a moderate position on fiscal matters, which would reduce the deficit through a package of reductions in both spending and entitlements, as well as increases in taxes.

Conservatives

This is the most right-wing faction within the Democratic Party. Although encompassing a broad set of ideologies, conservative Democrats are on the whole in favour of reducing taxes and adopting a conservative approach to social policies, which respects traditional Christian values. Their numbers grew hugely following the 2006 Democrat electoral victories. They have since achieved considerable success in watering down the eventual 2010 Healthcare Act, through securing withdrawal of proposals for a government public insurance option and by obtaining a commitment from Obama to introduce an executive order banning federal funding of abortions in return for their support. However, the retirement of a number of longstanding members of the Blue Dog Coalition in the run-up to the 2012 election, including one of its most conservative members Ben Nelson of Nebraska, shows the degree to which they are a declining influence within the party. Indeed recent commentators have suggested that they are a dying breed, especially given that they have reduced in size from a peak of 54 members after the 2008 election to just 14 members in the 113th Congress. Current conservative Democrats include:

- Georgia Representative **John Barrow**, who is a leading member of the Blue Dog Coalition. He was one of the 34 representatives who voted against the 2010 Healthcare Act and is a strong advocate for gun control, having achieved an endorsement by the NRA in his 2012 Senate race.
- North Carolina Representative **Mike McIntyre**, who was rated by the American Conservative Union as one of the 'most conservative Democrats' in 2012. He was one of only three Democrats to vote for Repealing the Job-Killing Health Care Law Act in 2011.

Party decline or party renewal?

The claim by one political commentator at the beginning of the 1990s that 'parties are in full retreat' shows the key debate for this topic, which centres on how far parties have retained power and influence within the American political system. Some commentators point towards the changing role of parties, which has led to a decline in their key traditional roles: selecting candidates, fundraising, communicating with

Examiner tip
With success from both liberal and conservative groups within the Democratic Party in recent years, it is worth keeping up to date with current news in America to judge the ascendancy of each group. In particular, consider the shifting ideology of Obama's presidency and the influence of various factions within the party.

Executive order A legally binding directive given to the federal bureaucracy by the US President. These orders state how federal agencies and officials should interpret congressionally established laws or policies. They thus allow presidents to guide and direct the implementation of congressional laws.

Knowledge check 8
Name at least five specific factions in each of the two main parties.

the electorate and developing policy. However, others have suggested a renewal of party power, given that they still retain a large degree of control over these areas and have developed a stronger leadership, along with a greater degree of partisanship and coordination, in recent years.

Evidence of party decline

Primaries

The increasing use of primaries in selecting candidates has given less power to party leadership to shape the direction of the party. This was best seen by the successful Tea Party infiltration of some Republican target seats in 2010, which were eventually lost to Democrats. However, the Blue Dog Democrats have also faced challenges from more liberal opponents in recent primary elections, such as the defeat of Pennsylvanian representatives Jason Altmire and Tim Holden who were criticised by liberal activists for their opposition to the new healthcare law and climate change legislation. In addition to this, the divisive nature of primaries encourages inter-party rivalry; as seen by the battle between both Clinton and Obama and Romney and Santorum during the presidential primaries of 2008 and 2012 respectively.

Limits on funding

Limits on party fundraising and expenditure have been introduced by the recent campaign finance laws. These have allowed presidential candidates to secure federal funding independent of the parties. Also, the 2002 BCRA (Bipartisan Campaign Reform Act) placed a ban on soft money.

Pressure groups

Pressure groups have replaced parties in communicating with the electorate, mobilising voters and developing policy. The rise of 527 groups and Super PACs, which are proliferating because of their ability to collect unlimited amounts of money, is one example of this. The *Washington Post* claimed that 80% of Romney's advertising spending in the 2012 presidential race came from Super PACs, such as the $104 million spent by 'American Crossroads'. Similarly, other groups have been established, such as the NRA Political Victory Fund and Moveon.org, to mobilise the electorate and encourage them to vote for certain candidates at election time. Finally, pressure group 'think tanks' are also increasingly undertaking policy development and exerting influence on the policy direction of the main parties. In this way, the liberal Centre for American Progress has been claimed to be the keystone of the Obama administration, and a *Time* magazine article from 2008 claimed that 'not since the Heritage Foundation helped guide Ronald Reagan's transition in 1981 has a single outside group held so much sway'.

Evidence of party renewal

Control over the nomination process

The parties have attempted to recapture the nomination process through the introduction of superdelegates, although the degree of influence they exert, in comparison to pledged state delegates, is debatable. However, the close 2008

Democratic presidential primary race did lead the *Guardian* to refer to the 795 superdelegates as the 'most powerful people in American politics'.

In addition, party control over the nomination procedures has been upheld in a series of Supreme Court rulings regarding the timing of primaries, as highlighted by the disqualification of Florida and Michigan in 2008 for violating Democratic Party rules.

Party structure and leadership

The parties have developed national party structures and leadership since the 1970s, which has served to strengthen their position. In particular, the Brock reforms led to the establishment of a permanent headquarters for the Republican National Committee.

Fundraising involvement

Parties are still involved in important fundraising activities, particularly through the establishment of various campaign committees to assist the election of party candidates. The 2012 elections set new records for party spending, with the Democratic National Committee spending over $319 million, while the Republican National Committee spent more than $404 million.

Control of the political agenda

Greater coordination of the party in Congress has given more power to the party leadership to control the political agenda. In particular, the House Speaker has increasingly managed to dominate the selection of committee chairs and membership. This was seen in December 2012 when House Speaker John Boehner conducted a 'purge' of Republicans who had failed to support his position on the fiscal cliff from key committee posts.

Party support

With the increasing partisanship of American politics seen from the 1990s onwards, some commentators were arguing that the electorate itself has become more and more polarised. With this in mind, it is possible to identify certain voting trends and groups which are inclined to vote for the Republican or Democratic Party. These are set out in Table 6 and Table 7.

Republican Party support

Table 6 Summary of Republican Party support (including % vote according to the NBC News exit poll of the 2012 presidential election)

Group	Reasons for support
High-income business professionals, with income over $250,000 (55%)	• Republican fiscal conservative views have always been appealing to this group • Republicans' widespread support for Grover Norquist's Taxpayer Protection Pledge, and their efforts to prevent increases to the rate of taxation for those earning over $250,000, secure this group's support

> **Examiner tip**
> Evidence of party renewal can also be found in the greater degree of partisanship among the two main parties. Therefore, in your essay answers you need to spend time reviewing the degree to which the parties are similar and different and how accurate it is to refer to the Democrats as 'liberal' and the Republicans as 'conservative' (see earlier headings).

> **Examiner tip**
> If a question asks about which groups tend to vote for a particular party, and why, make sure that your answer relates to specific groups and their motives for voting in a certain way. Use specific examples of policies which these groups would find appealing. No reward will be given to a review of party factions or policies which are not related to voting groups.

Examiner tip

For short-answer questions, such as those on why groups tend to vote for a particular party, it is best to develop three or four points fully in separate and distinct paragraphs. Avoid trying to cram in too many points, which would leave little time to explain each one. Make sure each point is supported by a relevant example.

Group	Reasons for support
White southerners	• The historic breaking of the Democrat Solid South, over black civil rights, has created a Republican stronghold in this area • This dominance is linked to the success of the Republican Southern Strategy, which targeted disaffected white southerners, and to the high degree of church attendance in many of these 'bible belt' states (see Protestant Christian groups below)
Rural voters (61%)	• Many favour the limited government regulation supported by the Republicans and especially their general opposition to gun control. This was shown by their distrust over Joe Biden's moves towards pushing for greater gun controls after the recent massacres in Aurora and Newton
Protestant Christians (57%)	• They support the traditional moral values espoused by socially conservative Republicans • This would include their opposition to abortion, as seen by the House Republicans' overwhelming support for a measure to cut off federal funding to pro-abortion group Planned Parenthood in 2011. Similarly, it was a Republican-controlled Congress which passed the Defence of Marriage Act (DOMA) in 1996
White males (62%)	• Many white males tend to prefer the Republican position on social policies. They are particularly opposed to the support among many Democrats for affirmative action and a relaxation of immigration laws • This was clearly shown by the 2012 Democratic platform, which advocated a 'comprehensive immigration reform that brings undocumented immigrants out of the shadows...in order to get on a path to earn citizenship'

Democratic Party support

Table 7 Summary of Democratic Party support (including % vote according to the NBC News exit poll of the 2012 presidential election)

Group	Reasons for support
Low-income working class, with income under $30,000 (63%)	• Many are unionised members who favour the more interventionist approach of the Democratic Party, such as Obama's auto bailout of car manufacturers • The Fair Minimum Wage Act 2007, raising the federal minimum wage from $5.15 to $7.25 per hour, shows the party's commitment to this low-earning group
Gays and lesbians (76%)	• They favour the Democrats' more liberal stance on social policies, and general commitment to gay rights • Obama made clear his support for same-sex marriage and praised the Supreme Court rulings on DOMA and Proposition 8

Group	Reasons for support
Latinos (71%)	• Although they are drawn to the traditional moral values espoused by the Republican Party because of their largely Catholic beliefs (and were effectively targeted by George W. Bush in this way), Latinos tend to be loyal as a minority group to the Democrats and are particularly attracted by their less hostile views on immigration • The Democrats have looked to offer some illegal immigrants a path to citizenship, in order to court the Latino vote • In contrast to the above, some Republican-controlled states have introduced strict immigration laws, fuelling fears of racial profiling among the Latino community, and some have called for a policy of 'self-deportation', by making their lives so uncomfortable that they are forced out of America
Unmarried women (67%)	• Support is strongest among single young women who particularly favour the party's more pro-choice stance on abortion • NARAL Pro-Choice America has been deeply critical of what it deems as the Republican House's 'war on women', with attempts to restrict women's right to choose
African Americans (93%)	• Historically this group has been the party's most loyal constituency, with the numbers voting Democrat rarely falling below 90% • The Democrats' position on upholding civil rights and more interventionist approach to government, with much greater support for affirmative action, maintains this support

Knowledge check 9

What is the difference between pro-life and pro-choice views?

Minor parties

For most commentators the USA is a two-party system, in which third parties face a range of obstacles to success. On a national level, third-party success has been very limited, although they have had some impact on the political system. The reasons for their lack of success are manifold. In some ways this lack of success is a product of the fact that the factions within the major parties allow them to cover a broad range of support, leaving little room on the political spectrum for minor parties. Primaries have also made infiltration of the main parties easier than challenging them, as best highlighted by the rise of Tea Party Republican challengers in the 2010 midterms. However, there remains a range of other obstacles to minority party achievement.

Two-party system
A system in which two major parties secure the vast majority of the vote during public elections and thus dominate nearly every elected post. These parties will thus control the legislature and executive between them.

Obstacles to success

First-past-the-post electoral system

The use of this winner-takes-all system, which is exacerbated by the Electoral College, makes it very hard for minor parties, which do not have both widespread national support and regional strength in depth, to succeed. In this way, George Wallace secured 45 Electoral College votes with 13% of the vote in 1965, targeting

What is the Electoral College?

southern states, while in 1992 Ross Perot achieved no Electoral College votes despite polling nearly 19% of the national vote.

Ballot access rules

State ballot access laws can be particularly stringent, soaking up the time and resources of minor parties. States such as California require a petition signed by 10% of the votes cast in the previous gubernatorial election, which amounted to over 1 million signatures for 2012.

Limited funding

The provision of federal matching funds in presidential elections works against minor parties, which require at least 5% of the previous vote for partial funding and 25% for full funding. In addition to the fact that this sets the bar too high for third-party candidates, with only three having achieved this since it was introduced, it also means that candidates, such as Perot in 1992, do not actually receive funding in the election cycle where they have had success. Given the huge cost, and restrictions, for getting on the ballot, as well as the lack of federal funding, minor parties find themselves in a 'catch-22' situation. They find it hard to raise money from pressure groups and PACs because they are unlikely to win. In 2012, Barack Obama raised over $715 million while Gary Johnson, the most successful minor-party candidate, raised just $2.5 million.

Co-optation

Co-optation The process by which major parties adopt the successful policies of minor parties in order to neutralise their opposition.

The major parties in the USA, through co-optation, often act as 'sponge parties', absorbing the successful policies of minor-party candidates, thus nullifying their electoral success. In this way, Perot's commitment to financial policies which would balance the federal budget was rapidly absorbed by both Clinton and congressional Republicans.

Lack of media coverage

Given the obstacles mentioned above, minor-party candidates find it hard to secure any print or TV news coverage. In addition, they are usually excluded from the national presidential debates, because of the requirement that candidates poll 15% with voters across five national opinion polls. Only Ross Perot in 1992 and John Anderson in 1980 have appeared in a presidential debate.

Impact of minor parties

Despite the lack of success in gaining electoral representation, many minor parties have still had an indirect impact on the US political system. This has been achieved on the one hand through influencing the political agenda and pushing certain issues towards the forefront of elections. An example is Ross Perot's success in 1992, which forced the major parties to focus on the issue of the budget deficit. Although he achieved no Electoral College votes that year, his policies were adopted by both Democratic President Bill Clinton and the Republican Congress, which achieved victory in 1994 with its commitment to a balanced budget as part of the Contract with America. As a result, the USA had a budget surplus by the end of Clinton's presidency.

Minor parties have also on occasion had an indirect impact on the eventual outcome of the election. This was most obviously the case in the 2000 presidential election, which swung on the result in Florida. Here Nader, who polled nearly 100,000 votes, arguably cost Al Gore the election when Bush achieved victory in the state by a margin of only 537 votes, meaning he ultimately won the Electoral College by just five votes, despite losing the overall popular vote.

Examiner tip

Be careful not to get drawn into detailing the impact or successes of minor parties in short-answer questions which only ask for factors which limit the success of minor parties.

Knowledge summary

- Appreciation of the ideological transformation of the two major parties from the broad non-ideological coalitions of the 1950s and 1960s into the more ideologically cohesive parties of today.
- Understanding of the extent of partisan politics in the USA, through evaluation of how far the two main parties are different from one another, and consideration of the influence of different factions within each party.
- Recognition of different groups of voters who typically support the two main parties, and the historical and contemporary reasons for this support.
- Knowledge of the arguments for party renewal or party decline, including an awareness of the debate around the extent to which parties remain relevant within the current political system, and how far they have come to be replaced by other bodies such as pressure groups.
- Knowledge and understanding of the factors which limit the success of minor parties, as well as the impact they have had on the US political system.

Pressure groups

The role and influence of pressure groups is at the very heart of discussion and debate about the democratic nature of the US political system. Despite the Founding Fathers' distrust of 'factions', the intricate system of checks and balances and separation of powers meant that they in fact created a system open to external influence — one that enables and positively encourages the formation of pressure groups. The constitution created a number of access points, at both state and federal levels, along with a political system that encouraged political participation and an active citizenry, in order to better hold politicians to account. As a result, America today has a wide range of pressure groups, each actively involved in the political process and attempting to influence government in order to shape policy outcomes in its own interests.

The first aspect of this topic is therefore concerned with the *methods used by different pressure groups to attempt to influence the system,* and how far they are successful in achieving their aims. The range of access points has generated debate about the relative success of different pressure groups and their ability to influence public policy at federal and state levels. To some commentators, the sheer size or financial wealth of certain pressure groups gives them a distinct advantage over other smaller and less affluent groups. Similarly, there is the issue of the prominence of different pressure groups, in which some are able to achieve a disproportionate influence over the political system due to their insider status.

Linked to this is the second question of *whether pressure group activity is healthy to US democracy,* or whether it undermines the democratic values of electoral

Access points The openings in the political system which pressure groups use to try to advance their aims. In the USA there is a range of such openings available to pressure groups, within the executive, legislature and judiciary, at both federal and state levels.

Knowledge check 11

Explain the US system of checks and balances and separation of powers.

accountability and 'one person, one vote'. There is a view, embraced by many liberals in particular, that money has come to dominate the US political process. This view that the US system is one in which 'you've got to pay to play', and where wealthy individuals and groups can manipulate the political system to their own advantage, is a powerful one. The rising cost of US elections, with the 2012 election reportedly costing more than $6 billion, has led many more liberally-minded political commentators to argue that the system benefits the rich at the expense of the poor. In contrast to this, in a nation which constitutionally enshrines 'freedom of speech' and encourages political participation, pressure group activity can be seen as fundamental to the values of the USA. Indeed, for many conservative commentators, pressure group activity should be left unconstrained by excessive federal regulation, while individuals should be free to engage in the political process without restrictions from federal government. They would argue that pressure group activity is beneficial for democracy and that it encourages a healthy competition between different groups, and actually prevents the accumulation of too much power in the hands of a few. Therefore, another key feature of this topic is to understand *the contemporary debate between those who believe pressure groups create an **elitist** power structure in the USA and those who believe they are fundamentally good for democracy* in creating a pluralist system of participation and compromise.

Range of pressure groups

The USA has a huge number of pressure groups, which represent a variety of issues and interests. There are a number of reasons to account for the existence of such a plethora of groups. The main reasons are listed below.

Access points

There are a large number of access points open to pressure groups in the US political system. The federalist nature of the US system enables groups to advance their interests to the executive and legislature at both state and federal levels. Alternatively, they can challenge decisions in the courts, organise the introduction of direct ballot initiatives or try to influence the outcome of pre-election primaries.

Expanding federal government

With an expansion in the size of federal government and the degree of regulatory control over businesses, a number of groups have sprung up to advance the interests of businesses, consumers and workers alike, in order to try and shape the policy framework to their advantage. Accordingly the **US Chamber of Commerce** claims to represent the interests of more than 3 million businesses, while the **AFL-CIO** combines 57 trade union groups, representing over 12 million workers in the USA.

Increasing partisanship

Arguably the ever more adversarial character of US politics has contributed to the growth of ideological and issue-based pressure groups. There has been a growth in the number of partisan think tanks such as the **Heritage Foundation**, which aims to 'build a stronger, more vigorous conservative movement', or the liberal **Centre for American Progress**, which in contrast is committed to 'progressive ideas and actions'.

Pluralist The idea that political power is shared among a broad range of groups which scrutinise each other and compete for influence. In this unit it refers to the idea that pressure groups hold government to account between elections, encourage political participation, and ensure all views in society are represented.

Knowledge check 12

What are pre-election primaries?

Similarly, the ideological divisions over a range of social issues have led to the creation of divergent pressure groups. Thus while **NARAL Pro-choice America** champions a woman's right to abortion, the **National Right to Life Committee** works against measures which allow abortions.

Scrutiny

Growing distrust of government has led to the growth of public interest groups designed to improve political scrutiny, as well as issue-centred groups looking to inform the electorate about the voting records and policy positions of politicians. In this way, the **Centre for Responsive Politics** tracks the influence of money and lobbying activities on elections and public policy making. Likewise the **League of Conservation Voters** publishes a biennial 'Dirty Dozen' report of those politicians with the worst environmental track record, 11 of which were defeated in the 2012 election cycle.

Methods and strategies

The huge number of access points open to US pressure groups means that they have a range of strategies available to them. The tactics used by individual pressure groups, however, will depend on a number of factors, such as their size, the funds at their disposal and which access points are open to them at any point in time. Thus those which are larger or better funded will be able to use a greater spread of tactics to target all three branches of the federal and state government. In contrast, other groups which cannot gain insider status will be forced to adopt more direct action outside the political system, such as mass protesting and public relations stunts, to gain publicity and media coverage. Nevertheless, there are a number of main strategies open to US pressure groups to enable them to influence state and federal lawmakers and/or executives.

Electioneering

Given the vast number and frequency of US elections, pressure groups are presented with a range of opportunities to take part in the electoral process, in an attempt to affect the outcome or shift the policy positions of candidates. Perhaps the two key areas in this respect are through the provision of funding to candidates, either directly or indirectly, and through endorsements and 'get-out-the-vote' activities.

Funding

Much of the electioneering in the USA is paid for by countless pressure and advocacy groups. These groups all seek to influence how voters look at the candidates, and thus indirectly shape opinions about a political candidate or party, without necessarily mentioning a specific candidate or instructing people how to vote.

The significant growth of these funding vehicles, responsible for collecting and allocating money on behalf of a range of individuals and pressure groups who share common interests, has arisen following the introduction of electoral funding laws. They have become a means through which pressure groups can maximise their funding power. Alternatively, with later developments such as 527s, they have arisen from exploiting loopholes in the funding regulations system; this has allowed

Examiner tip

Examiners will not expect, or welcome, long-winded explanations of the different types of pressure groups in the USA. The best answers will be able to demonstrate a wider knowledge of pressure group activity in the USA which does not rely solely on examples from those groups which are popular among all candidates, such as the NRA or NAACP.

Examiner tip

Make sure you are aware of a range of methods and strategies used by pressure groups, and ensure you have specific examples of how these strategies have been employed recently by different pressure groups in the USA.

them to circumvent the restrictions, following successful legal challenges about the constitutionality of such funding regulations.

Political action committees (PACs)

Political action committee An umbrella organisation which collects money from many lobby groups, and individuals, who are all concerned with the same issue. It uses these funds to support the campaign finances of sympathetic politicians and other advocacy groups.

Following the **Federal Election Campaign Act 1974** (FECA), which limited campaign donations to candidates, the number of political action committees (PACs) mushroomed, as they offered a way around this legislation. Although the maximum contribution to a PAC was $5,000, donations could be made to an unlimited number of PACs. The Federal Election Commission recorded that as of 2012 there were nearly 4,600 PACs registered in the USA.

The rise of these PACs has contributed to the growth of electoral expenditure and arguably given greater influence to pressure groups that are able to pool donations and support. Although it is hard to evaluate the degree of influence that is exerted from these campaign contributions, there have been some notable examples to suggest they go some way to influence the decisions of lawmakers.

Knowledge check 13

What are the limits imposed on individual contributions to a candidate under the FECA of 1974 and how did this change with the BCRA of 2002?

- In the 2 months following the Newtown shooting the Federal Election Commission disclosed that the **NRA** had raised $2.7 million through its PAC. Furthermore the **Sunlight Foundation** highlighted how 42 of the 45 senators who subsequently opposed gun control measures in 2013, to extend background checks on those purchasing firearms, received funds from gun lobbyists. The NRA alone had contributed over $800,000 to 40 of those senators over the previous 23 years.
- In 2009 the pressure group **Mobilization for Healthcare for All** led a protest against Democratic Senator Joe Lieberman, whom it accused of trying to undermine attempts to secure a 'public option', or government-funded health insurance, in the healthcare bill. It claimed his stance was shaped by his acceptance of more than $1 million in campaign contributions from the medical insurance industry during his time in the Senate.

527s

527s Technically 'independent' groups which collect unlimited 'soft money', which they use on voter mobilisation efforts and advertising. In reality they favour a specific campaign, by supporting or criticising a candidate's views or voting records on an issue.

Following the Bipartisan Campaign Reform Act (BCRA) in 2002, which effectively meant that PACs could no longer directly fund adverts which support or oppose a candidate, a number of 527 groups began to appear. These pressure groups circumvented the 2002 regulations by not using 'magic words' to expressly advocate a candidate's election or defeat. Though they have come to be eclipsed by Super PACs they still play a role in voter mobilisation efforts, by encouraging people to register to vote and to get out and vote. It may seem to be non-partisan, but the location and group focused on is usually very partisan. Thus the liberal **EMILY's list** spent nearly $10 million in 2012 through its 527. This targeted a key Democrat-voting group with the funding of its 'WOMEN VOTE!' program, which mobilised women voters in 22 races across 17 states.

Super PACs

Knowledge check 14

What is the difference between 'hard money' and 'soft money', with regards to campaign finance?

The Supreme Court decision in *Citizens United* v *FEC*, in January 2010, and the *Speechnow.org* v *FEC* ruling by the US Appeals Court, in July 2010, both served to lift many spending and contribution limits. As a result there has been an explosion of Super PACs, which can raise unlimited amounts of money to influence elections. Although these PACs must publicly disclose their finances, and they cannot coordinate with candidates or parties, they are free to advocate directly for or against a candidate. Though the impact of this is again hard to judge, especially given that 70% of all reported independent spending in 2012 was by conservative groups largely supporting Republican candidates, the statistics from the 2012 election are staggering:

- As of July 2013, a total of 1,310 groups had organised as Super PACs.
- Super PACs have raised over $828 million, spending over $609 million on the 2012 election cycle.
- The top two Super PACs of 2012, the conservative **Restore our Future** and **American Crossroads**, between them spent more than $246 million on the election.
- The *Huffington Post* claimed that 67% of all Super PAC donations in 2012 came from just 209 donors. Billionaire Sheldon Adelson, along with his family members, reportedly contributed £53.69 million to conservative Super PACs in 2012.

Endorsements

Pressure groups can also look to exert influence through the mobilisation of members and supporters to vote for a candidate. This is particularly effective where members are single-issue swing voters or are present in sufficient numbers in key battleground areas. Thus the **NRA Political Victory Fund**, which grades and endorses candidates based on their voting records, is seen as particularly influential. It claims that in 2008 it succeeded in 203 of the 271 congressional races it was involved in, as well as having an 84% success rate in endorsing state legislative candidates.

Lobbying

Lobbying is the process through which pressure groups seek to build relations with lawmakers to secure favourable policy outcomes and influence the legislative agenda. With 12,411 registered lobbyists in 2012 and with 'K Street corridor' becoming the centre for Washington-based lobbyist firms, it is clear that lobbying is now a 'persuasion industry' in its own right. Indeed in 2012, the US Chamber of Commerce employed 183 lobbyists, who spent $136 million on lobbying activities. The impact of lobbyists on the 2010 Healthcare Act shows the influence of lobbyists on Capitol Hill. These include the following:

- The Sunlight Foundation highlighted how 20% of the campaign funds for Max Baucus, former chair of the Senate Finance Committee, was contributed by lobbyists linked to **PhARMA**, representing the wealthy pharmaceutical industry. Some argue that this influenced his decision to exclude from initial discussions about healthcare reform in 2009 those pressure groups demanding wider healthcare coverage.
- In 2009, according to a study by the Center for Public Integrity, more than 1,750 companies and organisations hired about 4,525 lobbyists, who spent around $3.3 billion in order to influence the healthcare issue. This translated as eight healthcare lobbyists for each member of Congress.

Grassroots activism

The growth of the Tea Party movement, since its birth on 15 April 2009, over criticism of President Obama's economic policies, healthcare plans and 'big government' initiatives, shows the power of grassroots movements. A well-timed demonstration, such as the 1963 March on Washington by various civil rights groups, can help put

Examiner tip
Many of the examples of pressure group strategies to target the executive and lawmakers could equally be used to provide evidence that pressure groups are damaging to democracy. Certainly many of the examples of pressure group funding and lobbying activities could be used to support the argument that the system is fundamentally elitist and dominated by money.

Grassroots activism
Activities undertaken by ordinary members of pressure groups, which are seen to be free of party political control. The main forms of activity are marches and demonstrations aimed at raising awareness of issues among voters and politicians.

pressure on Congress, or push an issue onto the legislative agenda. However, it may also be seen as a sign of pressure group weakness, or as a last resort for groups which are unable to gain insider status.

Ballot initiatives

Examiner tip

Be careful not to claim that the Tea Party influenced politics prior to 2009, when it began. Many students wrongly refer to Sarah Palin as the 2008 vice-presidential candidate who was supported by the Tea Party. Though she later attached herself to this movement this was not until the 2010 midterm elections.

Pressure groups unable to shape the picture at a federal level, or wishing to target state governments, can use the federalist nature of the USA to achieve their aims. With 24 states currently allowing **initiatives** and **propositions**, which put proposed laws onto the ballot at election time, pressure groups are provided with a powerful way to influence the political system through direct democracy. Thus pressure groups can exert influence through using their membership and resources to:

- **introduce ballot initiatives** — gathering the signatures needed, and promoting the measure, to get it placed on the ballot
- **coordinate a campaign** — establishing campaign offices and funding full-time staff, such as public relations firms
- **fund a campaign** — running advertising campaigns and producing promotional material
- **staff a campaign** — providing grassroots support and volunteers to generate support or opposition to an initiative

There have been some prominent examples in recent years of pressure group success in this area, most notably over the issue of same-sex marriages and affirmative action. Examples include the following:

- **EqualityMaine** led the efforts to collect 85,000 signatures in order to get '**Question 1**' on the ballot in the 2012 election, allowing same-sex marriage in the state. In the run-up to the vote it was reported that proponents of the initiative were raising 36 times the level of funding as opponents, with Mainers United for Marriage raising $359,000 in comparison to the $10,000 raised by Protect Marriage Maine. In the end the measure succeeded in overturning a previous initiative which banned same-sex marriage in 2009, with nearly 52% of the vote.
- In 2008 **Proposition 8** was passed in California, which banned same-sex marriage. This saw over $82 million spent by various pressure groups, although interestingly those opposing the ban spent $4 million more than their opponents. There were also questions raised about the Utah-based Mormon church flooding the state with around 80–90% of the early volunteers and, according to Protect Marriage, contributing nearly half of the $39 million they raised.

Knowledge check 15

What methods can pressure groups use to exert influence through initiatives and propositions?

However, it is worth noting that in 2010 all six of the ballot measures in Colorado failed and in 2012 the **Florida Property Tax, Amendment 4**, providing tax relief for homebuyers, failed despite being the most heavily advertised measure on the ballot, with Realtors groups spending $4.7 million to support it.

Influence on the federal government

This aspect of the course looks at why each of the three federal branches of government offers different opportunities for pressure groups to advance their interests and thereby influence the political process. As well as the broad range of methods and strategies (outlined earlier) which are open to pressure groups in targeting members of the executive and legislature, there are a number of reasons why pressure groups might choose to target a specific branch of the government in order to achieve their aims.

Legislature

As the chief lawmaking body in the USA, Congress is an obvious target for pressure group activity. Attempts to build relations with members of Congress, through electioneering and lobbying, are part of the staple diet of many pressure groups. Indeed, securing the passage of legislation is a powerful way for pressure groups to gain influence over the political process. This is helped by the fact that the political system provides numerous access points and opportunities for pressure groups to influence the course of legislation through Congress. Of particular significance are the following:

- **Bicameral legislature:** As the USA has a bicameral legislature it means that pressure groups can use both the House of Representatives and the Senate to influence and shape legislation as it passes through either chamber.
- **Divided government:** The two chambers of Congress are often held by different parties, as was the case after the 2010 midterms, giving a pressure group a greater chance of at least watering down legislation it disapproves of.
- **Committee system:** The power of congressional committees, as the 'gatekeepers' to legislation, provides opportunities for pressure groups to shape or block legislation before it arrives on the floor of Congress.

There are also reasons why pressure groups might choose to focus their efforts on one of the chambers.

House of Representatives

As the House was given the exclusive power to initiate money bills, this makes it a significant target for groups wishing to secure a slice of the colossal annual federal budget, or those wishing to influence where that money is spent. In this way since the Republican Party gained control of the House following the 2010 'Tea Party tidal wave', the House has voted on 37 separate occasions to repeal 'Obamacare', with the most recent vote seeing all Republicans and just two Democrats support the measure. Certainly the on-going budget negotiations of 2013 show the influence of conservative groups on the House, with many Tea Party Republicans making clear their willingness to block any budget which raises taxes or provides funds for 'Obamacare', raising the threat of a government shutdown in the USA.

Senate

The exclusive powers of the Senate make it a similar target for other pressure groups, especially given its powers in the following three areas.

Foreign policy

With the constitutional power to ratify treaties, which requires two-thirds of Senate support, the Senate is a target for many groups wishing to influence America's foreign policy position. Many commentators have pointed towards the power and insider status gained by the **American Israel Public Affairs Committee** (AIPAC). Indeed, following AIPAC's 2013 annual convention, which was addressed by Vice-president

Examiner tip

As the course does not require an in-depth understanding of local and state-based politics, questions in this topic tend to focus on national access points. Therefore it is important to know how, and why, pressure groups use different methods for each branch of government and also to have relevant examples to judge the degree of success they enjoy.

Bicameral legislature

A system of government in which the legislature is divided into two chambers. All bills must pass through both chambers, before being signed by the president, in order to become laws.

Knowledge check 16

Name two reasons why pressure groups might seek to influence the US Senate.

Joe Biden, Senator Barbara Boxer introduced the US-Israel Strategic Partnership Bill into the Senate, which aimed to cement relations between the two nations.

Confirming appointments

The Senate is also responsible for confirming, by a simple majority, presidential appointments to many positions in the executive branch and, more importantly, to all posts in the federal judiciary. In recent times, the process of Supreme Court nominations has become increasingly politicised. Some argue it is dominated by pressure group activity, especially since the controversial rejection of Robert Bork, President Reagan's nominee in 1987, who was subjected to a series of attacks from liberal interest groups such as the **National Organization for Women** (NOW) and the **National Abortion Rights League**.

Filibuster A senator's right to unlimited debate, unless 60 senators vote to bring debate to a close. This gives individual or groups of senators the power to delay or prevent a vote on a bill they disagree with.

Filibuster

The Senate's unlimited right to debate is also a factor in many pressure groups' decisions to target individual senators, who can exert real power with the mere threat of a filibuster. In 2013 the **Safe Communities, Safe Schools Act**, which aimed to widen gun control in the USA, was successfully blocked by the threat of a filibuster, when a concerted lobbying effort by pro-gun groups meant it failed to reach the threshold needed to bring debate to an end on the Senate floor.

Executive

As with the legislature, pressure groups in the USA are presented with two main options when looking to influence the executive. They can choose to target the president and his team of advisers directly, using many of the tactics outlined above. Alternatively, they can look to influence the federal bureaucracy, especially if they find the president is less than receptive to their views.

Examiner tip

Good answers to questions about the influence of pressure group activity on the executive will mention both the direct impact on the president as well as the indirect influence on the federal bureaucracy. Thus you should look to include a review of the influence of lobbying, electioneering, endorsements and grassroots activities, as well as the impact of iron triangles and regulatory capture.

President

Although the system of checks and balances severely restricts the degree of presidential power, the president still holds a considerable amount of power, especially in setting the national legislative agenda. The president's position in moulding the legislative direction of the USA, through the annual State of the Union address and his powers of persuasion, can be used by pressure groups to achieve their aims. Similarly, pressure groups can encourage the president to use his executive orders to change the direction of policy, such as with the constant reinstatement and reversal of the 'Mexico City Policy', which bans federal funding for family planning clinics that give abortion advice. George W. Bush satisfied pro-life groups by reinstating the policy in 2001. In contrast Obama initially reversed this policy, before passing executive order 13535 in 2010, which again removed federal funding for these groups, as part of a compromise to get 'Obamacare' passed by Congress.

Federal bureaucracy

For those groups not ideologically supported by the president, there is still the opportunity to target and build relations with the relevant executive departments and regulatory bodies. Civil servants may well have long-term agendas which do not fit with the president's immediate priorities, allowing pressure groups access to try and shape policy and thwart the president's will. When this relationship involves the relevant congressional committee, an **iron triangle** (see 'Controversies and criticisms' on p. 43) can develop, which holds a firm grip on policy that presidents find hard to break. Similarly, pressure groups will look to develop relations with the relevant regulatory body which is supposed to be scrutinising them. When this develops into too cosy a relationship, there can be **regulatory capture** (see p. 44), in which the 'watchdog' becomes the 'lapdog', as the pressure group exerts influence over the regulatory body charged with regulating it.

Judiciary

There has been much criticism of the Supreme Court's power of judicial review, with some commentators describing the justices as 'politicians in robes' due to the fact that many of their constitutional rulings are in effect judicial lawmaking. For this reason, and whether the criticisms are warranted or not, groups in the USA are uniquely positioned to influence judicial decisions in two main ways:

- **Litigation:** Funding test cases to the Supreme Court is a way in which pressure groups can secure a ruling which is favourable to their interests. The **American Foundation for Equal Rights** used the courts to challenge Proposition 8, which had banned a same-sex marriage law previously passed by the California state legislature. In the landmark *Hollingsworth* v *Perry* ruling the Supreme Court effectively overturned the ballot initiative by not allowing those traditional marriage activist groups, which had placed it on the ballot in 2008, to defend it in court without the support of state officials.
- **Amicus curiae:** By presenting legal briefings to a court which is undertaking judicial review, a pressure group would hope to sway the court's decision in its favour. These briefings have increased by over 800% since the 1940s, with 98 being filed in the 2013 *Fisher* v *Texas* ruling, by pressure groups such as the **National Association for the Advancement of Colored People** (NAACP).

In addition, as mentioned above, pressure groups look to mould the overall makeup of the Supreme Court by influencing a president's choice of nominee or the Senate ratification process. Indeed the withdrawal of George W. Bush's nominee Harriet Miers in 2005 was seen as the product of a concerted campaign by conservative pressure groups, such as Christian Rights groups, which were worried about her position on a series of social issues.

Power of pressure groups

Overview

This topic looks at the debate surrounding the power and influence of pressure groups, and how far their activities and actions are damaging to US democracy. On the one hand, pluralists would argue that they are a sign of a healthy democracy through encouraging participation, scrutiny and engagement in the political process. However, others point towards their elitist nature, which allows a few, usually wealthy, pressure groups to dominate the system.

Examiner tip

The issues of both iron triangles and regulatory capture are relevant to the methods used to influence the executive, but are also part of the controversies and criticisms surrounding pressure group activity. They support the idea that certain pressure groups have an unjustified and unhealthy influence over the political system.

Amicus curiae The right of individuals or groups to present information to the court, in order to help the justices make their decision before a ruling is made. The term refers to a legal briefing which summarises a pressure group's standpoint on the legal issue being considered.

Examiner tip

Always check the focus of pressure group questions. Too often students are quick to reproduce a pre-planned essay on the elitist and pluralist arguments without specifically relating their points to the question set. This is especially the case when students are asked about the influence of pressure groups over issues, or the polarising effects of pressure group activity.

Knowledge check 17

Explain how the *Lawrence v Texas* and the *Windsor v US* rulings extended the constitutional protections given to gays and lesbians in the USA.

Positive view of pressure group activity

The first key argument is that pressure groups provide a healthy 'free market' of opinion, and give empowerment to all US citizens, who are able to use them as vehicles for influencing their political leaders. Many conservatives would point to the array of access points, which give multiple opportunities for everyone to be heard and make a contribution to shaping society.

There is strong evidence that the actions of pressure groups have in the past protected minority groups, who might be expected to be excluded from an elitist system. The role of black civil rights groups, such as the NAACP, in securing legislative equality with the passage of the Voting Rights and the Civil Rights Acts, along with their influence in dismantling the southern system of segregation, through *Brown* v *Board of Education*, are two cases in point. Similarly both the 2003 *Lawrence* v *Texas* ruling, funded by **Lambda Legal**, and the 2013 *Windsor* v *US* case, which was supported by the **American Civil Liberties Union**, extended the constitutional protections given to gays and lesbians in the USA.

Limitations and constraints

Other commentators would further point out that the system works to limit existing barriers which stop full participation. In their view, the system of regulations and constraints placed on pressure groups prevents them from becoming too powerful, or dominating the system. In particular, they would point towards the following examples:

- **Federal Election Campaigns Act 1974:** restricted the influence of wealth by setting limits for individual donations and establishing a system of federal funding for major party candidates.
- **Bipartisan Campaign Reform Act 2002:** tightened the restrictions from the previous act by regulating soft money and introducing advertising restrictions.
- **Lobbying Disclosure Act 1995:** widened the requirements for lobbyists to register their activities while also banning the giving of gifts.
- **Honest Leadership and Open Government Act 2007:** attempted to close the revolving door (see page 43) by introducing a 'cooling-off' period after leaving office, while also extending the ban on gifts and requirements for full disclosure of lobbying activities.

Negative view of pressure group activity

The alternative view is that America is dominated by a power elite, and that efforts to try and constrain the power of pressure groups, to ensure there is a level playing field in which all groups have the same opportunities, have failed. Thus, for certain political commentators, the wide range of access points can be exploited only by those groups with the resources and wealth to take advantage of them. In this way, certain pressure groups have come to dominate, using their greater numbers or wealth to monopolise the political system. As a result, commentators contend that smaller groups are unable to exert any real political power as they do not have the wealth, voting power or insider connections to secure the ear of those in power. Evidence for this argument can be found in the influence of funding and lobbying on the political system, as well as in the existence of three main areas of controversy in the USA:

- revolving-door syndrome
- iron triangles
- regulatory capture

Controversies and criticisms

Revolving-door syndrome

A high proportion of lobbyists have come from the ranks of former politicians, or staff members — 64% of those members of the 112th Congress who failed to get re-elected in 2012 moved into the lobbying industry. This leads to the accusation that US politics is dominated by an insider elite, whose members are able to influence the political system through the 'revolving door', which gives them constant access to those in power.

Furthermore, critics also point out that this creates situations where politicians are unduly influenced, in creating public policy, by the lucrative prospect of a high-paid job for a lobbying firm when they leave politics. There are many examples of this overlap between those in politics and lobbying:

- **Peter Davidson**, a former adviser to then-House Majority Leader Dick Amey, and **Tom Tauke**, a former Republican congressman, both now work for Verizon Communications. They were instrumental in securing clearance for a multi-billion-dollar deal with cable companies in 2012, following a Department of Justice investigation into the monopoly status this would create.
- Senator **Jim DeMint** left his South Carolina Senate post in 2013 to take up a role as the president of the influential Heritage Foundation.
- **John Ashcroft**, who served 6 years in the Senate and 4 years as the US Attorney General, set up the Ashcroft Group upon leaving office. In 2005, less than a month after collecting $220,000 from Oracle Corporation, John Ashcroft used his contacts to secure a multibillion-dollar acquisition contract for Oracle with the Department of Justice.

Iron triangle

An iron triangle is a political community featuring three very powerful players in the political process. When pressure groups, congressional committees and the federal bureaucracy have shared aims, they can develop a very strong relationship. This gives them an iron grip on public policy, enabling them to effectively dictate and block attempts by Congress or the president for reform. Perhaps the most criticised iron triangle has been the **military industrial complex** (MIC), the strong relationship between the Defense Department, the congressional armed forces committees and the leading weapons manufacturers, which some argue has contributed to the USA's huge defence budgets. The following case serves as an example:

- Attempts to save $2.5 billion from the defence budget in 2012, by cancelling contracts for a drone programme provided by the defence manufacturer Northrop Grumman, were thwarted by the company's lobbying activities. Its 26 lobbyists, packed with former congressional staff, successfully blocked the cancellation by

Examiner tip
The criticisms of pressure group activity can be grouped into five main areas, although there is significant overlap between them. You might refer to the earlier points regarding the dominance of money in the political system through pressure group funding and lobbying activities, as well as the points which follow regarding the insider status gained by certain groups.

Revolving-door syndrome The idea that the same people dominate public policy making. As many lobbyists are former politicians, or their aides, the view stands that the same people remain in the political world to control policy.

Knowledge check 18
What is lobbying?

Iron triangle A strong relationship between a pressure group, the relevant congressional committee and the relevant government department or agency in an attempt to guarantee the policy outcomes to the benefit of all three groups.

channelling over half a million dollars to members of the House Armed Services committee in the 2012 election cycle. In addition to this it came to light that they had provided $113,000 since 2009 to its chairman, Buck McKeon, who wrote an influential letter to the newly appointed Defense Secretary Chuck Hagel in 2013 reminding him of the commitment to continue funding the drone programme.

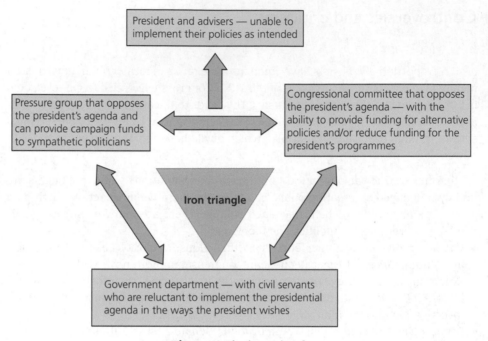

Figure 1 The iron triangle

Regulatory capture

A close relationship between regulatory agencies and the pressure groups that they are supposed to be overseeing can mean that government watchdog agencies often turn into lapdogs. This has been a recent criticism laid at the door of the financial and energy regulatory bodies, in the wake of the recent banking crisis and the Gulf of Mexico oil disaster. This is evidenced by the following:

- A **Securities and Exchange Commission report** in March 2008 pointed towards its own failures in regulating the financial sector with a system which allowed banks to 'opt in or out of supervision voluntarily'. Many blamed the heavy lobbying from all five big investment banks in 2004 for this voluntary system.
- The 2010 **Interior Department review** into the Gulf of Mexico oil disaster found that it resulted from the failed regulation of those who were supposed to be policing the nation's offshore drilling facilities.

Knowledge summary

- Knowledge and analysis of the issue of pressure group influence and how far such groups act as democratic vehicles for participation and scrutiny or merely serve to further entrench the position of a wealthy, influential minority.

- Understanding of the range of access points available to US pressure groups, and evaluation of how far this creates an open system in which all are able to engage in the political process, or how far this allows large, wealthy groups to dominate.

- Understanding of the range of methods available to pressure groups in influencing the different branches of federal government, as well as ability to judge the success with which pressure groups are able to advance their agendas.

- Awareness and appreciation of the debate around the extent to which pressure groups' power is a good thing, including the elitist and pluralist arguments based around the extent to which money and insider connections allow certain groups to dominate the system.

- A solid understanding of the various regulations placed upon pressure group activity and contemporary criticisms of their actions.

Racial and ethnic politics

The 1776 US Declaration of Independence declared that 'all men are created equal'. This was a fundamental principle upon which the Founding Fathers based the US political system. Part of this topic surrounds the contemporary American debate about the extent to which the history of racial discrimination, and lack of opportunities for significant racial and ethnic minorities, means that *equality for all has been, and remains today, a distant dream for significant numbers of African Americans and Latinos*.

The history of publicly-sanctioned discrimination, which effectively removed the civil rights of many racial minorities, has led many to question whether the USA is a genuinely meritocratic society. For many liberal commentators, the product of this history of racial discrimination is the continuing existence of institutional racism and lack of opportunities for racial and ethnic minorities. They would point towards the fact that these minorities remain at an inherent disadvantage with regard to their lack of economic progress and educational attainment. Conservative commentators, in contrast, argue that the USA has rid itself of racism and is today a **post-racial society**, in which there is a true equality of opportunity for all. They point towards the increasing economic achievement and affluence among minorities as well as their growing political success.

The second aspect of this topic is the political debate surrounding *the strategies to remedy these past historical injustices*. As can be expected, many conservatives do not feel there is any justification for, and fundamentally disagree with, any attempt by the government to introduce measures to rectify these historical issues of discrimination. For many liberals, however, this ignores the responsibility of the American government to remedy the problems. Liberals point towards the political and moral responsibility of the US government to redress the continuing barriers to educational and economic achievement facing minorities.

A final aspect of this topic is to consider the *current debate surrounding immigration reform*, which has increasingly come to the forefront of contemporary politics with the growing importance of the Latino vote in US elections. In particular, students will need to be aware of the *reasons for this debate and the alternative reforms suggested*. Many conservatives see immigration reform as strictly an issue of controlling immigration

Institutional racism
The idea that racism is embedded in many US organisations. It may not be overt racism, but it leads to the indirect disadvantage of minorities through selection or promotion procedures which perpetuate racial and ethnic stereotypes. Thus, for example, many minorities are seen to struggle to achieve university places compared to their white peers.

Examiner tip
You need to understand the divide between liberal and conservative opinion about whether the USA is truly equal and how far racism still persists. For maximum marks, aim to provide a balanced answer which includes specific evidence of equality and minority successes as well as evidence of inequality and the ongoing barriers which racial and ethnic minorities face.

and securing US borders from illegal immigrants. For them the focus should be on sealing the US border with Mexico, to prevent further illegal immigration, while also adopting a more proactive approach among law enforcement personnel to finding and deporting undocumented aliens working in the USA. In contrast liberals claim that immigrants are people with rights who are essential to a failing economy, and who therefore should be encouraged to integrate with US society through a nationwide amnesty programme. They support measures, such as the DREAM act, which would give these undocumented aliens a pathway to citizenship.

History of inequality

Despite the intentions of the Founding Fathers to create a political system which would protect and uphold the core values of individual liberty and equality of opportunity, the history of the USA is one in which the constitution enshrined slavery and excluded Native Americans from the rights given to the white, Anglo-Saxon, Protestant Americans (WASPs).

Constitutional protection of slavery

Although the US Constitution does not explicitly uphold slavery, it did implicitly authorise it. Indeed, constitutionally, slaves — who did not retain voting rights themselves — were originally counted as three-fifths of a person in the apportionment of seats to the House of Representatives and Electoral College; this resulted in the southern slave-owning states being significantly over-represented. In addition, the 1857 *Dred Scott* v *Sandford* ruling by the Supreme Court ruled that slavery was not only constitutionally permissible but could not be limited to the southern states.

Abolition of slavery

Although the American Civil War, and the 13th Amendment, banned slavery, this did not lead to the end of racial discrimination for African Americans, particularly in the former slave-owning states. Here black people saw the erosion of their right to vote, and a system of state laws were passed, known collectively as **Jim Crow laws**, which enforced segregation and in effect made black people second-class citizens. Again this was given constitutional protection by the Supreme Court, which ruled in favour of 'separate but equal' facilities in the 1896 *Plessy* v *Ferguson* case.

The southern states continued to deprive African Americans of their basic civil rights by establishing a system which disadvantaged black people politically, socially and economically. Furthermore, their position was perpetuated by a segregated public education system, in which African-American schools received significantly less funding. Even those blacks who moved north did not always find their position improved. Many still faced informal segregation, lack of economic opportunity and a hard life in black ghettoes.

Civil rights

A series of civil rights movements, protesting against racist laws, swept across America from the 1950s onwards. Two key events acted as a catalyst for these

Examiner tip

With essay questions for this topic, avoid long descriptions and narratives about the history of racism in the USA. Remember it is not a history essay; you must answer the question set by the examiner and relate points to the political debate in America today.

protests: the *Brown* v *Board of Education* Supreme Court decision and the Montgomery bus boycott. The 1954 Supreme Court verdict, which overturned *Plessy* and declared the practice of school segregation unconstitutional on the grounds that it was 'inherently unequal', acted as a spur to civil rights campaigners. Similarly, the challenge to segregation on Alabama's bus network, which began with the arrest of Rosa Parks, a black woman who refused to vacate her seat for a white man in 1954, had wide-reaching consequences and gave birth to the Civil Rights movement.

While the passage of the Civil Rights Act 1964 and the Voting Rights Act 1965 marked the end of these protests, by outlawing the state-based practices of formal and informal discrimination, questions still remain about how far this marked an end to discrimination for racial minorities in the USA. This question of ongoing discrimination also lies at the heart of the current debate about how far America has, and whether it should even look to have, erased this history of racial discrimination and 'inherited guilt'. This feeds into the contemporary debate about the extent to which the USA is now an equal country, in which every race and ethnicity can succeed.

Continuing inequalities

Many liberals point towards the continuing existence of inequalities in the political, social and economic life chances of minorities to suggest that minorities, especially those from Latino and African-American communities, are at a fundamental disadvantage in modern America. For them, the fact that many minorities remain under-represented at nearly every level of government, that there are more than twice as many blacks and Latinos living below the poverty line as whites, as well as the vast differences in educational attainment between ethnic and racial groups, are evidence of these ongoing inequalities.

Evidence of political inequalities

The lack of political representation for minority groups can be seen as evidence that there exists a fundamental difference between the dream of equality of opportunity and the political reality that exists in America today. There is a strong argument among many liberals that the barriers to minority political achievement demonstrate the failings of the American political system, which favours the wealthy white establishment at the expense of minorities. The following can be cited in support of this argument:

- Despite black people accounting for 13% and Latinos for nearly 17% of the US population, in the 113th Congress their share of the seats in the House was only 9.4% for African Americans (41 members) and 7.8% for Latinos (34 members).
- There are only two Native Americans in Congress — Illinois Representative Tom Cole and Oklahoma Representative Markwayne Mullin.
- Only eight African Americans and nine Latinos have ever served in the US Senate.
- Much of the minority political representation in America is secured as a result of preferential redistricting and the creation of majority-minority districts, such as the Latino 'earmuff district' in Illinois, rather than race-less voting.

Knowledge check 19

What is the full name of the pressure group which funded the *Brown* v *Board of Education* case in 1954?

Examiner tip

Always check questions to see whether they refer to issues of equality and opportunities facing *all* ethnic and racial minorities, including Latinos, or whether they refer only to African Americans. Remember you will get no reward for knowledge and analysis which does not focus on the question.

Examiner tip

A solid structure for answering questions about equality, and lack of opportunity, for racial and ethnic groups is to weigh up evidence of success and continuing problems using the headings set out here. You could look to spend two paragraphs on each of these areas, thus evaluating how far there is equality *socially*, *politically* and *economically*.

Evidence of social problems

The life chances of many minority groups are seen to be severely limited, which would further suggest that minorities are at an inherent disadvantage compared to whites. It can be argued that the existence of institutional racism in the USA, especially within the education and criminal justice systems, continues to impact upon minorities today. Further examples of this enduring lack of social opportunity can be seen in the following:

- A 2013 report by the Education Trust found evidence of a 'glass ceiling' in the educational attainment of minority students. It highlighted a wide gap in attainment among fourth graders, with 1 in 10 white students achieving an advanced level in maths compared to just 1 in 50 Latinos and 1 in 100 African Americans.
- Recent data from the US census bureau shows a huge disparity in the levels of education among racial groups with just 8.2% of white Americans without a high school education compared to 16.2% of African Americans and 21% of Latinos.
- David R. Roediger, professor at the University of Illinois, referred to the 'highly racialised anti-crime political appeals' that caused a sevenfold increase in incarceration rates between 1975 and 2005. This has particularly affected minorities. A 2012 report by the American Civil Liberties Union (ACLU) found that while 1 in every 106 white males is incarcerated that figure is 1 in 36 for Latino males and 1 in 15 among African American males.
- Following the 2012 *Arizona v USA* ruling, regarding the controversial **Arizona SB1070** law, many argued that it still allows law enforcement officials to stop and search anyone suspected of being an undocumented immigrant, which will perpetuate state-sanctioned profiling. Even Obama's comments on the verdict echoed these concerns about racial profiling, when he stated that 'No American should ever live under a cloud of suspicion just because of what they look like'.

Evidence of economic disparities

In economic terms there still exists a huge variance in the positions of African Americans and Latinos when compared to whites. This is seen as a barrier to minority opportunity, and key economic data, including the following, highlight the prevailing problems.

- Recent unemployment rates stood at 13.8% for blacks, 9.7% for Latinos, but just 6.8% for whites.
- A 2013 report by the Institute on Assets and Social Policy (IASP) found evidence of a growing wealth gap between white and African-American families, which nearly tripled between 1984 and 2009 from $85,000 to $236,500.
- In 2013 the research group United for a Fair Economy, in its annual State of the Dream report, made startling claims about the wealth and asset disparities among racial groups. It found that minorities were struck harder by the recent recession, with the average net wealth of whites falling by just 6.7% compared to a drop of 27.1% among black families and 41.3% among Latinos. It also found that the net worth of white families is nearly six times as large as that of other minorities, and in particular they have over ten times more financial assets than black and Latino families.

Examiner tip

Your revision should ensure you have detailed knowledge to support your analysis with well-developed evidence. It is not enough to make broad generalisations about the problems facing minorities, for example by stating they have a higher unemployment rate. The best answers will provide precisely selected, detailed, and wherever possible the most recent, examples as evidence.

- A 2012 report, issued by the Centre for American Progress, found that 95.8% of Fortune 500 CEOs were white men with only 1.2% being Latino and 0.8% African American.
- The same report found that minority women held just 3% of the seats and there was not a single Latino female board chair of a Fortune 500 company in 2010.

Post-racial America

In an article in the *New Republic* in 2000, entitled 'Race Over', black Harvard professor Orlando Paterson claimed that race is no longer an issue in America, given the dramatic gains made by African Americans since the 1970s. In addition to those who argue that racial and ethnic minorities have made considerable progress, other, largely conservative, individuals point to the successes of other minority groups in the USA, which they refer to as 'model minorities'.

Evidence of political success

There is significant evidence of minority political representation across America, which gives weight to the view that America has extinguished the legacy of slavery and discrimination to become a truly colour-blind society.

- As well as Obama's successful bid for the presidency, there are a number of leading minority politicians such as the Attorney General Eric Holder and Latino senators Marco Rubio and Ted Cruz. The success of two African Americans in the 2012 elections was also notable — South Carolina's Tim Scott and Mo Cowan in Massachusetts.
- Presidential appointments have also given the Supreme Court a greater degree of racial and ethnic balance, with justices such as the African-American Clarence Thomas and Latino Sonia Sotomayor.
- At a state level, minorities have also made good progress. In 2009 Colorado, despite having only a 4% black population, became the first state in which both the state legislative leaders were African American. Similarly, in the Deep South state of Alabama, where 26.5% of the population is black, African Americans hold 23% of the seats on the state legislature.

Evidence of social advancement

In their 2003 book *No Excuses*, Stephan and Abigail Thernstrom argued that educational attainment is based largely on ethnic cultural factors. They refer to the positive work ethic of model minorities such as Asian Americans, when compared to the Latino and African-American communities, as a reason for varying achievement levels, rather than any lack of social or educational opportunities.

Further evidence of minority social advancement can be seen in the following:

- A 2013 Department of Education report showed the highest graduation rates among minorities since the 1970s, with 93.5% of Asian-American, 71.4% of Latino and 66.1% of African-American students graduating. Indeed research by the Pew Hispanic Centre found that in 2011 only 14% of Latinos dropped out of high school, half the level of 2000 (28%).
- In a 2007 article for the *New York Times*, Orlando Paterson argued that the disparity in black imprisonment rates may not be solely down to judicial bias or racism but

Model minority A minority ethnic or racial group which achieves a greater degree of success when compared to other groups. The term is usually used to identify the higher achievement of one ethnic minority group over another.

to the high rate of violent crime within the community — the rate at which blacks commit homicides being seven times higher than whites.

- A number of states have introduced policies to advance racial diversity in education. For example, the Texan Ten Percent Plan guarantees students who graduate in the top 10% of their high school class automatic admission to all state-funded universities.

Evidence of economic achievement

Knowledge check 20

What is meant by a post-racial America?

Despite variances in the degree of economic achievement, many conservatives argue that the existence of an increasingly affluent black middle class, as well as the success of many other minority groups, is evidence that there are no longer any barriers to economic achievement.

- According to a report by the Selig Center for Economic Growth, the buying power of minorities has grown hugely in the last decade with the Latino market accounting for $1.2 trillion in 2012 while African-American buying power increased by 73% between 2000 and 2012.
- The same report stated that there was a 61% increase in black-owned businesses in the 5-year period between 2002 and 2007.
- In 2010, 45.4% of blacks and 47.5% of Latinos owned their own home.
- Census data also show that between 1990 and 2009 the average household income for African Americans rose by $2,872, to $32,584, and by $2,514 for Latino households, to $38,039.

Affirmative action

Examiner tip

Ensure that you are clear on the attitudes of different groups towards affirmative action and also that you are able to evaluate its impact. For the exam you should understand all the arguments about whether the policies remain, or ever were, necessary, and be able to judge the extent of their success.

Affirmative action generally means giving preferential treatment to minorities in admissions to universities or employment opportunities for government and private businesses. More specifically, it refers to a range of policies originally developed to correct decades of discrimination and to give disadvantaged minorities a boost. Some say that the diversity of American society today, as opposed to that of 50 years ago, indicates that the programmes have been a success. In contrast, others, particularly conservatives, think the policies were never, or are no longer, needed and that they lead to more problems than they solve.

History of affirmative action

Since the passage of the Civil Rights Act 1964 and the Voting Rights Act 1965 some Americans have argued that the USA established a clear and legal framework for **equality of opportunity**, in that all races were now free from legal discrimination, ensuring de facto equality.

However, the focus soon shifted away from formal and legal equality towards more substantive equality. Many liberals argued that there was a need for **equality of outcome** to level the playing field for previously disadvantaged groups. For many, there was now a need for America to address the fact that African Americans in particular were at a historical disadvantage, as they lagged behind whites in terms of income, employment and educational attainment.

To those who supported substantive equality (including President Johnson), the 1964 and 1965 Acts were the beginnings, not the end, of a campaign for equality. A series of policies were adopted that became known as **affirmative action**. The measures established ranged from 'soft' measures to target job adverts at minorities to 'hard' measures which included giving quotas and preferences to these groups.

Restrictions to affirmative action

Affirmative action came under immediate scrutiny from those who were critical of what they deemed to be positive discrimination and an increase in federal government intervention. From the 1970s onwards the policies of affirmative action were opposed by those politicians and commentators who saw it as merely reverse discrimination.

In addition, since 1978, a series of Supreme Court decisions have gone some way to water down and limit the forms of affirmative action deemed constitutional, without explicitly declaring affirmative action to be unconstitutional. The most notable of these rulings are listed below.

- *Regents of the University of California v Bakke* **(1978)** accepted that race could be one factor, among many, in university admissions but could not directly disadvantage majority applicants.
- *Adarand Constructors v Pena* **(1995)** re-established the need for 'strict scrutiny' to ensure that federal affirmative action programmes had a specific purpose and justification.
- *Gratz v Bollinger* **(2003)** declared the University of Michigan's racial quota system of admissions unconstitutional as it was 'too mechanistic' in awarding all minorities 20 of the 150 points needed for admission.
- *Grutter v Bollinger* **(2003)** ruled that the University of Michigan's Law School admissions programme was constitutional as it used an 'individualised' affirmative action programme, in which race was only a 'plus factor'. Although it upheld as constitutional the continued use of certain affirmative action programmes, it did suggest that this may only be necessary for a further 25 years.
- *Fisher v Texas* **(2013)** did little to change the existing law and instead upheld the Bollinger cases and referred the matter back to the lower courts. Many commentators awaiting this decision had wrongly believed it would issue a definitive ruling of the constitutionality of affirmative action.

As well as Supreme Court rulings a series of initiatives and propositions in recent years has meant the issue of affirmative action's place in the USA has become further clouded. By 2010 at least five states had seen the successful introduction of measures to ban affirmative action, including **Michigan Proposal 2**, banning its use in public employment, education or contracting in 2006, and **Arizona Proposition 107**, which was passed by a vote of over 60% in 2010.

Arguments against affirmative action

- **Reverse discrimination:** Conservatives believe that the broad nature of affirmative action programmes, even without quotas, can lead to rich minorities being given preference over poor white applicants.
- **Lower standards and motivation:** A 2011 report, by the Education Trust, pointed out that within 6 years of enrolling for a degree, the graduation rates for

> **Knowledge check 21**
>
> How do the views of conservatives and liberals differ over the issue of affirmative action?

> **Knowledge check 22**
>
> Explain two key ways in which affirmative action has been restricted since its introduction in the 1960s.

> **Reverse discrimination**
> The idea that race-based affirmative action is racist in itself by actively disadvantaging white people. This is seen to be linked to the critical view of many Americans when using the terms 'positive discrimination' and 'racial preferences' for affirmative action programmes.

white students stood at 62% while it was only 51% for Latinos and 40% for African Americans.

- **Prevents a truly colour-blind society:** Some, like Supreme Court Justice Clarence Thomas, argue affirmative action is condescending and insulting; in fact he stated 'Any effort, policy or program that in some way accepts the notion that Blacks are inferior is a non-starter with me.'
- **Undermines minority achievement:** Too often, minority achievements are demeaned by affirmative action.

Knowledge check 23

What were the two Supreme Court rulings in 2003, regarding affirmative action, and what did they decide?

Arguments in favour of affirmative action

- **Promotes diversity:** In her dissenting opinion, in the 2013 *Fisher* v Texas ruling, Ruth Bader-Ginsburg wrote about the 'educational benefits of a student body diversity'.
- **Levels the playing field:** Given the huge economic and social disadvantages that many ethnic minorities face, affirmative action is seen as a way to ensure equality of outcome. Indeed it was highlighted by Bowen and Bock, in their book *The Shape of the River*, how race-based university admission practices can successfully advance the life chances of minority students.
- **Breaks down racial stereotypes:** The opportunities gained, directly or indirectly, through affirmative action have given minorities the chance to show they are every bit as capable as whites in a range of fields.
- **Compensation:** In the words of President Johnson, at Howard University in 1960, 'it is not enough just to open the gates of opportunity. All our citizens must have the ability to walk through those gates'.

Examiner tip

All students should look to have a solid understanding of the different views among critics and proponents of affirmative action. However, the best answers will also present the opinions of specific individuals, who may well have more moderate or conservative views of affirmative action.

Individual and group views on affirmative action

- **Nancy Pelosi, former Democrat House Speaker**, in a statement following the *Fisher* v *Texas* ruling, reaffirmed her support for affirmative action by stating that 'government entities must not be blind to the lingering effects of discrimination in the past'.
- **Barack Obama** said in 2009 that although 'crude quotas' were unconstitutional, he still supported, in certain circumstances, 'taking into account issues of past discrimination' and the role of affirmative action in ensuring the 'diversity of a workforce or a student body'.

- **Rand Paul, Republican Senator for Kentucky**, supports repeal of all measures and suggested in 2010 that private businesses should be free to choose employees without any restrictions, even if this could be deemed discriminatory.

Alternatives to affirmative action

Abolition

- There has recently been a strong push among American states to ban racial or gender preferences. Much of this has been a reaction to the controversial and unprecedented decisions in the Bollinger cases, sponsored by the conservative pressure group the **Centre for Individual Rights**. These cases effectively declared 'mechanistic' racial quotas unconstitutional, without specifically declaring affirmative action unconstitutional. In particular, the *Grutter* v *Bollinger* case, by a slender 5–4 majority, upheld affirmative action but stated that admissions must be flexible, and reaffirmed that they could not be crude quotas, because race must be considered as one among many other admission criteria.

- Many conservative groups, such as the **Center for Equal Opportunity**, call for a complete ban on all forms of affirmative action and have led attempts to legally challenge affirmative action.
- Florida governor, Jeb Bush, decided in 1999 to abolish affirmative action with his 'One Florida' initiative. Although this led to widespread demonstrations, conservatives would counter criticisms with the fact that over the decade from 1999 to 2009, total state enrolment among Latinos rose from 13.8% to 18%, while black enrolment remained relatively static at 13.6%.

Class- and income-based action

- Some opponents argue that affirmative action benefits middle- and upper-class minorities at the expense of lower-class Caucasians. Thus some argue that there is a need for class-based, or income-based, affirmative action which does not consider race or ethnicity. Writing in the *Washington Post* in 2012, Richard Kahlenberg, a senior advisor for the liberal think tank **The Century Foundation**, called for universities to 'vigorously pursue race-neutral alternatives such as socioeconomic affirmative action'. However, the **African American Policy Forum** believes that: 'Race-conscious affirmative action remains necessary to address race-based obstacles.'

School and cultural reform

- A number of largely conservative individuals argue that the inability of minorities to compete is because those minorities need to be 'Americanised' and encouraged to conform more closely to the mainstream cultural norms of the USA.
- The Texan Ten Percent Plan ensures that minority students are not competing with students from schools that are better funded and resourced. Since its introduction, total admissions of Latinos to Texas universities have jumped from 14% in 1996 to 24% in 2012.

Reparations

- Since 1989 Congressman John Conyers Jnr from Michigan has introduced a bill every year to study the case for reparations. He urges the federal government to undertake a thorough review which will lead to financial compensation to the descendants of African slavery.
- Though calls for reparations do not hold widespread appeal in America, the 'Millions for Reparations' march, in 2002, did see over 50,000 people descend on Washington DC.

Immigration

Immigration is becoming a critical and deeply divisive issue, especially given the growing importance of the Latino vote in many states along the Mexican border.

Quota A specific number or percentage of educational or work placements set aside for minority groups. Where the setting of quotas is too broad and 'mechanistic', a range of Supreme Court judgements have declared this unconstitutional.

Examiner tip
With questions that require an evaluation of alternative methods to ensure racial and ethnic equality in the USA, wherever possible refer to specific individuals or groups or provide examples of specific programmes which are available in the USA today.

Reparations
Compensation paid to individuals who have suffered from previous state-sponsored discrimination. In the USA there is debate about whether this should be in the form of a financial payment, made to the descendants of those who suffered, or through the provision of healthcare coverage.

Examiner tip

As this is a contemporary issue, you are advised to stay up to date on the latest news regarding immigration. A particularly good website is www. pewhispanic.org which has a range of articles and is a great source of information.

Amnesty A general pardon granted by a government, which would allow illegal immigrants to apply to become American citizens.

Given that there are an estimated 11.2 million, mostly Latino, illegal immigrants in the USA, there is a bitter divide over how best to tackle the situation. This is especially the case given the changing demographics in the USA, with the Mexican-American population growing by over 11.4 million in the last decade. On the one hand, conservatives see it as strictly an issue of controlling immigration and securing US borders from illegal immigrants. However, liberals claim that immigrants are people with rights who are essential to a failing economy, and who therefore should be encouraged to integrate with US society through a nationwide amnesty programme.

Immigration reform

Immigration reform has been a hotly contested topic in recent years. The measures for reform can be broadly grouped into those calling for an amnesty and those calling for greater border control and enforcement. A range of reforms have been attempted in recent years, the most notable of these include:

- **DREAM Act (since 2001):** This would have given citizenship to those who had been brought into the USA as minors and had subsequently graduated from high school and university or undertaken 2 years' military service.
- **Bush 'guest worker' scheme (2004):** This allowed a range of immigrants, in shortage areas, to gain temporary work visas.
- **Secure Fences Act (2006):** This aimed to improve border defences by building a 700-mile fence along the US border with Mexico, and widening other security measures.
- **Comprehensive Immigration Reform Act (2006):** This looked to both increase border security and provide a path to citizenship for long-term undocumented immigrants, while also extending the 'guest worker' scheme.

Amnesty

Some groups including the **National Council of La Raza**, the largest Latino pressure group in the USA, have called for a path to citizenship for the existing 11.2 million undocumented immigrants in the USA. This was the basis of a 2001 bipartisan **DREAM Act**. However, the bill which was passed by the House in December 2010 failed to overcome a filibuster led by Republican Senator Jeff Sessions, who argued that the bill amounted to a reward for lawbreaking.

More recently some in the Republican Party have looked to relax their attitudes towards immigration reform, especially in light of the party's poor performance among this demographic in 2012. Indeed in an article for the *Wall Street Journal*, on 2 May 2013, Republican presidential hopeful Marco Rubio was quick to defend his plans for a comprehensive immigration reform package, by stating that it would end de facto amnesty by recognising 'the reality that they are not going home'. However, the proposed **Border Security, Economic Opportunity, and Immigration Modernization Act** of 2013 met with continued criticism among conservatives such as Jim DeMint, the president of the conservative Heritage Foundation, who claimed the new proposals were merely 'another amnesty' that would be detrimental to the USA.

Border control

A number of conservatives continue to call for a greater focus on policing the borders, with tighter immigration laws requiring local law-enforcement officials to question those they suspect of breaking the law, and harsher penalties for those found employing undocumented immigrants. However, the recent *Arizona v USA* Supreme Court ruling severely restricted the Arizona SB1070 law, which looked to target these issues at a state level. This ruling limited the scope of state officials to tackle immigration and arguably gutted state-based legislation which looked to take a harsh line on immigration. The sensitive nature of this topic, which many argue strikes at the heart of states' rights, was seen in the verdict of Justice Kennedy, who wrote the 'State may not pursue policies that undermine federal law'. In response to the ruling Obama was quick to call for Congress to adopt a comprehensive, and national, immigration reform package as he claimed 'the patchwork of state laws is not a solution to our broken immigration system'.

Yet the continued partisan nature of this debate is highlighted by the fact that no action has been taken by the Obama administration against sanctuary cities that refuse to cooperate with the federal government on immigration matters. Indeed a spokeswoman for Attorney General Eric Holder said there was a difference between 'not enforcing federal law, as so-called sanctuary cities have done, and a state passing its own immigration policy that actively interferes with federal law'.

The increasing significance of this issue is highlighted by the fact that some have called immigration 'the new slavery', in the way that it has come to divide America. Thus future elections will in part be fought by those liberals who feel immigration is a national issue, and support the path to citizenship for illegal immigrants, and those conservatives who fear 'big government', and invoke the rights of states in deciding their own approach to dealing with immigration.

Sanctuary city A term given to a city which protects illegal immigrants. This is usually through the process of not enforcing federal immigration laws, by preventing police or municipal employees from inquiring about immigration status.

Latino political significance

The political impact of the Latino population has best been pointed out by the Pew Hispanic Center, which noted that the Latino vote in 2012 amounted to 10% of all voters. As well as this there are an estimated 8.3 million eligible, but unregistered, Latino voters, and roughly 50,000 new Latinos reach voting age each month in the USA. Overall Latinos are the largest single minority voting group, and the fact that there has been a 43% increase in the Latino population in America, between 2000 and 2010, means that they are clearly a rising demographic who look set to have an increasing share of the vote in future years.

A second factor which increases the significance of the Latino voting bloc is their concentration in many border and western states. This is also evidenced by the surging Latino population in southern states such as New Mexico, which saw its Latino population rise by 24.6% between 2000 and 2010, to 46.3%. In many crucial swing states such as Florida, Nevada and Colorado Latinos constitute between 20% and 46% of potential voters. Given that each of these states was won fairly comfortably by Obama in 2012 it would suggest that they are an important group for the main parties to target in order to secure electoral victory.

Examiner tip

Questions regarding the significance of the Latino vote overlap with the political parties section of the specification. In revision consider evidence from previous elections which show their significance as a core voting group, to either party, as well as any policies the parties adopt to appeal to them as a voting group.

Knowledge summary

- An appreciation of the extent to which race is deeply ingrained in the history and political values of the USA with its focus on fairness.
- A detailed evaluation of how far contemporary America can be viewed as a fundamentally equal society in which everyone, regardless of race or ethnicity, has the same opportunities to succeed.
- Understanding of the divide between those conservatives who believe that there are no longer any barriers to opportunity and those liberals who point towards the enduring legacy of discrimination which acts as an obstacle to minority success.
- Awareness of the continuing debate over the extent to which overt or institutional racism persists in the USA and the degree to which the problems faced by minorities are a result of personal and cultural factors which should be addressed within their own communities.
- Awareness of the controversy over the degree to which government should intervene to help minority groups, largely though affirmative action.
- Knowledge and understanding of the range of alternative strategies proposed to ensure equality of opportunity for all racial and ethnic groups.
- Understanding of the growing significance of Latinos and why immigration reform has become such a controversial political topic in the USA.
- Knowledge of the political divisions surrounding the issue of immigration reform and the range of suggested strategies in dealing with immigration.

Questions & Answers

How to use this section

At the beginning of this section there is an explanation of the assessment objectives and a guide as to how the marks for each assessment objective are distributed among the different questions on the paper. There follow some specimen examination questions. These are neither past examination questions, nor future examination questions, but they are very similar to the kind of questions you will face.

The best way to use this section of the guide is to look at each question and make notes on how you would go about answering it, including the key facts and knowledge you would use, relevant examples, the analysis, arguments and evaluations you would deploy and the conclusions you would reach. You should also make a plan of how you would answer the whole question, taking into account the examiner tip (indicated by the icon 𝐞) immediately below the question.

After each specimen question there are two exemplar answers. One will be a strong answer and the other will be either weak or of medium quality. The strength of each specimen answer is indicated in the examiner commentary (again indicated by the icon 𝐞) that follows it. In the commentary there are also notes on the answer's strengths and weaknesses and an indication as to how marks would be awarded for each assessment objective. Now compare these specimen answers with your own notes. Amend your notes to bring them to the standard of the stronger specimen. Having done all this, you can now attempt a full answer to the question, aiming to avoid the weaknesses and include the strengths that have been indicated in the specimen answers and explanations of the marks.

Of course you may use the information in your own way. The above guidance is merely a recommendation. Remember, however, that simply 'learning' the strong specimen answers will not help — these are answers to specimen questions, not to the questions you will actually face. It is preferable to learn how to answer questions 'actively', that is by writing your own answers, using the questions and answers as a guide. In this way you will be able to tackle effectively any questions that may come your way in the examination.

Assessment objectives overview

	AOI Knowledge and understanding	AO2 Analysis and evaluation	Synopticity	AO3 Coherent argument	Total
Short answer	5 marks	7 marks		3 marks	15 marks
Essay question	12 marks	12 marks	12 marks	9 marks	45 marks

Knowledge and understanding

Assessment objective 1 involves the breadth and depth of a student's knowledge, which must be relevant to the question being asked. Look to show knowledge of the key terms in a question through definitions and the correct use of political terminology.

In this way questions about criticisms of the presidential nomination process, for example, will need to show knowledge of frontloading, invisible primary, raiding, voter apathy etc.

Analysis and evaluation

Assessment objective 2 is concerned with the quality of your explanation and evaluation of the question set. In answering questions, stronger students will look to present a rounded argument which evaluates a range of factors and weigh up the value of individual factors.

In this way a question on the extent to which the Republican Party is dominated by conservatives, for example, will look to present a balanced argument. There will, however, be a clear judgement on the question and the basis for that judgement will be apparent.

Synoptic debate

Synoptic marks are *only awarded for essay questions*. They are awarded for considering at least two sides of an argument, although some questions will have a broader range of viewpoints. The obvious way to safeguard synoptic marks is to ensure you do not present an essay which is wholly or largely one-sided. You must look to show a very well-defined sense of opposing arguments.

In this way questions which ask, for example, how far race-based affirmative action has been a success and is still needed will require, as a minimum, viewpoints that it has *and* has not succeeded. However, more developed responses will consider the range of views among liberals that affirmative action must continue, be adapted or be replaced with more far reaching policies such as reparations, as well as the views of conservatives that affirmative action was never required in the first place or is no longer necessary.

Developing an argument

To meet the requirements of assessment objective 3, essay questions in particular will require the presentation of a range of views on an issue. However, in presenting and analysing these views your own line of argument must be indicated at the start, and be clear throughout. To produce a good coherent argument you must look to:
- **signpost your judgement** and the basis for it at the start
- **support your argument** by presenting the key factors which sustain your argument, using detailed and relevant examples as evidence to back up each point
- **unravel counter-arguments** by explaining the weaknesses of other viewpoints

This is not simply presenting a list of points for or against and summing up at the end. Examiners are looking for a sustained attempt to present and unpick different arguments on an issue.

In this way questions about the extent to which pressure groups weaken democracy, for example, will require an explanation of viewpoints that they do and do not weaken democracy. However, stronger answers will look to weigh up these views, in order to present a cohesive argument about whether they are positive or negative to the US democratic process.

Short-answer guidance

Timing is key for these questions as you are only given 15 minutes to respond. Thus these answers require you to immediately address the question, avoiding long-winded and descriptive introductions.

Also, ensure you read the question. There are no synoptic marks for short answers, so questions *do not* require a balanced response *unless* the question specifically asks you to address both sides or signals that you should with words such as 'to what extent' or 'how far' etc.

These answers are best addressed by focusing on fully developing three to four factors, in separate paragraphs, which answer the question set.

Essay guidance

You should look to spend 45 minutes on each essay question, but ensure you spend at least 5 of those minutes planning your response. The danger is that students jump into questions, having selected a topic, without understanding the requirements of a specific question.

You should also make sure you refer back to the question *throughout* your essay, so your answer does not drift away from it and lack coherence.

If you struggle with structuring your answer, make sure you get the basics right:
• Start with an introduction which sets out the debate and signposts your argument.
• Present three to four well-developed arguments for each side of the question, showing evaluation of each argument presented.
• Conclude with a summary of the question and clear judgement on the strongest argument and basis for its strength.

Question 1 Elections and voting

Assess the importance of National Party Conventions.   (15 marks)

ⓔ Most short-answer questions have a narrow focus and will only ask you, for example, to consider the 'strengths' or 'advantages' of an aspect of the political system. With these questions it is important not to stray into discussions of 'weaknesses' or 'disadvantages'. However, the word 'assess' in this question points towards the need for an evaluation of the significance of National Party Conventions, to consider the extent to which they have become meaningless and serve no purpose.

Student A

Originally National Party Conventions, before the existence of primaries, were used to choose the party candidate for the presidential race **a**. However, the use of primaries in particular has led to the decrease in importance of party conventions.

ⓔ A solid start which is well focused on the issue of importance and **a** provides a clear judgement, which also signposts the evidential basis for this, namely the rise of primaries.

Although the Convention officially chooses the party's candidate for the presidential race, since the use of primaries and especially since a process of frontloading, most obviously seen by the 2008 Tsunami Tuesday, delegates often know who the candidate is due to be in advance **b**. This is because other candidates drop out early on in the primary race, as candidates need an absolute majority to win. Thus in 2012 Rick Santorum suspended his campaign more than 19 weeks before the Republican Convention **c**. Thus it is clear that the National Convention merely rubberstamps the result of the primary race, and has very little significance **d**.

ⓔ Also a very focused paragraph, **b** this clearly establishes the line of argument from the outset that the formal and traditional role of the convention, in choosing a presidential candidate, has ended. More importantly, the student has identified what they view as the main reason for this change, specifically primaries and frontloading. The student goes on to **c** develop a detailed example from 2012, while **d** reinforcing their judgement that conventions are insignificant.

Similarly its role of defining the party platform **e** and generating serious debate about the direction the party should take has taken second place to just presenting a positive face to the media. As has the job of selecting the vice-presidential running mate **f**, which is also often known well in advance, and decided by the primary winner, rather than the party. With the party platforms being so vague it is clear that conventions serve very little practical purpose.

ⓔ The student does well to identify two other factors which they judge have diminished the importance of conventions, that of **e** defining a party platform and **f** selecting the vice-presidential candidate. However, this answer could be further improved by supporting these points with examples, such as the fact that Romney announced his choice of Paul Ryan 15 days before the 2012 Convention.

However, this is not to say they are insignificant as they do give an opportunity to create unity within the party after months of divisive campaigning. This is currently one of the most important and growing informal aspects of the National Convention as it is important to 'fire up' not only the party faithful but ordinary voters **g**. It is a moment where unity is important, as seen in both 2008 conventions when Clinton spoke of her support for Obama and when McCain chose Palin to help energise his conservative faithful **h**. Similarly, the media coverage and 'bounce' in the polls acts as a springboard into the election campaign. Certainly the success of the 2004 Republican Convention, held in New York after 9/11, led to a bounce of 2% which gave the Republicans a significant lead in the polls.

ⓔ Here the student shows that they are 'assessing' the question by clarifying the level of their judgement in recognising that conventions remain important in creating party unity. They specifically relate this to the informal functions of conventions in **g** enthusing the core party members, as well as **h** the political role of appealing and presenting a united front to the electorate.

Despite this, it is clear that the formal roles of the conventions are no longer important and it now merely serves as a media circus with an attempt to present a positive face of the party **i**. It has sacrificed serious political debate and discussion for media coverage and false unity before the presidential election.

ⓔ This is a clear and concise conclusion, which clearly **i** reiterates the student's judgement on the question. It confirms the strength of the answer.

Overall this answer makes three well-developed points, which are all supported by relevant and detailed examples, about **b** the lack of a formal role in selecting the presidential candidate, and **g** the informal roles of enthusing the party faithful and **h** appealing to the electorate. It is also credited for mentioning the two points, albeit less well developed, about the insignificant role of conventions in **e** defining the party platform and **f** choosing the vice-presidential candidate. The clear level of structure, in which each point is well developed in separate paragraphs, and the fluency of the communication make it a very strong response, which would achieve a good A grade in the exam.

14/15 marks awarded.

Student B

National Party Conventions are held once every 4 years when there is a presidential election. It is a meeting of the main delegates of a party who choose the presidential candidate **a**. Both parties hold conventions following the results of the party primaries and their functions are to choose the presidential candidate, unite the party, develop a platform and announce the vice-presidential candidate **b**.

ⓔ This is a solid opening, which shows an understanding of **a** what National Conventions are and **b** the functions they fulfil. However, it is a very general and descriptive paragraph which does not fully signal the student's intention to 'assess' importance, instead focusing on what conventions do.

There is debate, however, as the increased use of primaries, since the 1970s, as opposed to caucuses, has been criticised as demeaning the importance of National Party Conventions **c**. The main reason for this is because the use of primaries means that the presidential nominee is often known well before the convention **d**, thus its main function is obsolete. However, as witnessed in 2008, the winner is not always clear. Barack Obama and Hillary Clinton fought a bitter battle up to the convention, where the superdelegates ultimately made the final decision **e**.

(e) The second paragraph more clearly **c** links to the question of importance, by **d** pointing out the impact of primaries in reducing the formal role of selecting the presidential candidate. Although these points are well made, they lack a relevant example, and **e** the attempt to assess the question by weighing up the importance of the 2008 election is slightly flawed, given that Clinton conceded to Obama on 7 June, more than 2 months before the Democratic Convention.

On the other hand, the National Party Conventions provide an important role of uniting a party **f**. With infighting from the party throughout the primaries, rifts can occur and divide the party's core. Thus the Conventions boost morale behind the winning candidate by uniting the party through the discussion of party policies and gathering support from those who might be doubtful. The image of a united party is essential for winning the presidency. In 2012, for example, Mitt Romney used the Republican Convention to put aside splits with other candidates **g**.

(e) This shows a good attempt to assess and balance the student's response to the question **f** by looking at the conventions' role in securing party unity. It also rightly suggests that this is a result of the need to heal the wounds and rifts rising from the primary campaign. Again, however, it does not fully develop its evidence to support this argument, with **g** the example from 2012 lacking specific detail on the ways in which they were divided during the primary process, perhaps by the success of Rick Santorum who won support among core social conservatives or the appeal of Ron Paul, who appealed to the libertarian wing of the party.

The choice of the vice-president is also not a role any longer of the convention as the president chooses this beforehand by trying to balance the ticket **h**. He chooses a candidate who complements his own weaknesses and this is announced well before the convention, such as with Obama and Biden. Therefore it is apparent that National Party Conventions remain important within the role of presidential nominations and, with the phenomenon of frontloading and primaries, their function to unite the party has grown in importance **i**.

(e) The conclusion is confused in its structure by **h** presenting another relevant point regarding the lack of importance in choosing the running mate, while **i** at the same time trying to summarise the student's judgement that conventions do play an important role in uniting the party.

This lacks structure and development, but given its solid knowledge and attempt to address the question, it would achieve a strong C grade in the exam. It makes three reasonably developed points, but they are not always well supported by detailed examples. Although the student shows a sound understanding of the question, they do not fully 'assess' the importance of conventions and the examples given are not always relevant or sufficiently developed.

9/15 marks awarded.

Edexcel A2 Government & Politics

Question 2 Political parties

Explain the key policies pursued by the Democratic Party in recent years.   (15 marks)

(e) This question is focused on the need to explain fully a range of policies that the Democratic Party has pursued recently, which can include both those that it has proposed and those that it has actually passed. Students must focus specifically on the Democratic Party, and the question makes specific reference to 'recent years' indicating that the examiner is expecting the knowledge and examples to be contemporary and current.

Student A

The Democratic Party is seen to be the more liberal party. This is as a result of its social policy. For example, during the Clinton presidency, he advocated for welfare, seeing it as a 'second chance' **a**. More recently Obama passed the Patient Protection and Affordable Healthcare Act, which reformed welfare provision in the USA by federally mandating the purchase of healthcare, and had almost overwhelming (all but 34) support from the rest of the Democratic Party **b**.

(e) Although this answer starts with a dated, and rather vague example, in which the student **a** refers to the attempted healthcare reforms under President Clinton, this introduction quickly backs up its initial point **b** with reference to a more recent example. Indeed this example shows a very good knowledge of the provisions of the policy to introduce a federal mandate.

The Democratic Party sees importance in civil rights on the social side of the political agenda. In regards to civil rights, Democrats have traditionally followed policies which favour equality. For instance, gay rights, which have been upheld by the repeal of 'Don't Ask, Don't Tell' **c**, allowing homosexuals to serve in the armed forces, and in Obama's recent support for same-sex marriage. This has been more widely seen in the Democrats' commitment to introduce the 'Respect for Marriage Act' allowing same-sex couples the same federal benefits as heterosexual couples **d**.

(e) The second point is well focused on developing specific social policies that have been passed or advocated by the Democratic Party. In particular the student shows a strong understanding of its commitment to gay rights with the passage of both **c** DADT and the reference to **d** the issue of same-sex marriage.

Economically the Democratic Party has shown its liberal Keynesian economic policies in the recent budget negotiations on the back of the threatened sequestration **e**. In their dealing with the House Republicans the Democrats have looked to support further fiscal stimulus plans, such as Obama's Jobs plan, as well as supporting increasing taxes for the most wealthy in society, such as measures to raise taxes for those earning over $100,000 **f**.

(e) This paragraph makes a third well-developed point. This means that the answer is already looking at 11+ marks. **e** The student is explaining the economic stance recently adopted by the party in the January 2013 budget negotiations. Again the point is well supported with **f** a range of contemporary examples.

> Taking the more liberal and moderate policies into account, it is also key to address some of the main conservative factions within the Democratic Party, which come from Congressmen such as Ben Nelson **g** (who is leading the Blue Dog Democrats). The policies of these conservative Democrats take a more traditional view towards marriage and the family. It was this faction that led to Obamacare being watered down **h** showing the Democrats' policies are not all liberal.

ⓔ The conclusion is a little less strong than the rest of the answer but does at least recognise that the Democratic Party does not exclusively follow a liberal agenda. **g** Mention of Blue Dog Democrat Ben Nelson neglects the fact that he did not stand for re-election in 2012, while **h** the point about their success at watering down Obamacare may refer to the agreement to secure an executive order which would remove federal funding for abortions, but is less convincing then previous points. Time could have been better spent developing a specific policy area that the majority of the party has supported rather than just setting out the existence of this faction.

This strongly focused answer, which uses a broad range of recent, comprehensive and relevant examples, would ensure this student achieves an A grade. Overall it is an excellent answer that clearly addresses the question and explains a range of recent Democratic policies.

13/15 marks awarded.

Student B

> The Democrat Party follow traditionally very liberal policies and believe in new modernist ideologies like advocating gay rights and promoting women. One policy Democrats pursue is gay rights as they believe all citizens have the constitutional right to marry whatever their sexuality **a**. One of the Democrat Party platforms for the 2012 presidential election was the idea of gay marriage. Gay vote for Obama was 91% **b**. The Democrats value equality for women and the women's vote is very important for Democrats. In 2012, women voted Democrat 57% rather than 43% for Republican **b**. The Democrats' policies for women are more appealing as they are generally pro-choice and promote equal pay for women, such as the recent Lilly Ledbetter Act **c**, to give women better pay.

ⓔ This is a long introduction which, despite setting out the general liberal agenda of the party, does not start very well. In particular the **a** initial point about the party's support of gay rights is very general and does not give a specific policy that it has advanced towards this aim. Similarly this point, and the second one which sets out the party's position on equality for women, **b** drifts into references to the voting pattern of these two groups, rather than focusing on the policies the party is pursuing. Despite this both points are rewarded, and **c** the second point is supported with mention of the fair pay act that was passed by the Democrats in 2009.

The Democrat immigration policy is a strong value which attracts ethnic minority voters. The Democrats promote the idea of immigration in their party platform and call for immigration reform. Obama has called for a path to citizenship for ethnic minorities, called the DREAM Act, which attracts the Latino vote **d**. In the 2012 presidential elections ethnic minority vote for the Democrats increased which showed the party policy can appeal to the Latino vote because the Republicans call for higher border patrols which can put off Latino votes and make them seem out of touch to voters **e**.

ⓔ This second paragraph is much more relevant to the question and **d** begins to outline a specific immigration policy. Despite this the answer still drifts into **e** irrelevant references to voting groups, rather than focusing on the question set.

Overall, unlike the Republican Party, the Democrats follow policies which are less traditional, as they support gay rights **f**. Latinos are traditionally Christian but Republican candidates **g** can ruin chances of getting the ethnic minority vote because of people like Mitt Romney who in 2012 suggested ethnic minorities self deport.

ⓔ This is a vague conclusion, which adds little to the answer. It merely summarises the points made earlier **f** and again drifts into **g** irrelevant mention of how voting groups are liable to shift over to support the Republican Party. The student could have given a specific policy to support equal rights for gays, such as the repeal of 'Don't ask, don't tell' in December 2010.

Overall this is a solid response showing some sound understanding of the general policy position of the Democratic Party, and would be strong enough to achieve a C grade in the exam. However, it could be much improved. It needs to be more focused on the question set while also fully supporting its points with relevant and contemporary examples.

9/15 marks awarded.

Question 3 Pressure groups

To what extent is size the most important factor in explaining the success of pressure groups?

(45 marks)

ⓔ Essay questions often begin with 'To what extent…' or 'How far…'. This is a signal that you must cover both sides of a question, i.e. how far it is and is not the case, while also having a clear judgement and line of argument throughout. In this instance the question asks you to analyse the importance of size in pressure group success, but better answers will be expected to consider and weigh up a range of factors and have a clear line of argument about which is the most important in contributing to pressure group success.

Student A

Pressure groups in the USA are successful for a range of factors, but in democratic terms it is arguable that many are successful by virtue of their size. However though a group may have a lot of support this does not mean that its level of success in achieving its goals will be proportional— the political priorities of the government and the amount of funds at a pressure group's disposal are also likely to influence its success and are perhaps more critical **a**. However pressure groups regardless of their success act as a crucial way for the views of 315 million individuals to be articulated **b**. That said it is clear that the size of a pressure group is less important than the influence of money, what Ted Kennedy said was 'the best Congress money can buy', and the insider status gained by small groups who reflect more the political priorities of the government of the day **c**.

ⓔ This introduction starts with a clear focus on the question and effectively **a** sets out a range of factors which account for pressure group success. However, it is not faultless and the reference **b** to the democratic importance of pressure groups is not entirely relevant to the question. Indeed, although the answer does successfully draw back to the question at the end of the introduction, **c** by signposting the student's judgement that size is not the most crucial factor, this paragraph does not make clear which of these two alternative factors is, in the student's judgement, the more crucial to pressure group success.

Despite this it cannot be discounted that size is still an important factor for pressure group success as it allows a group to have a large base of support from which to make its request. Large membership size acts as a source of legitimacy and influence for certain pressure groups — the American Association of Retired Persons (AARP) has 35 million members. The AARP is able to influence political bodies by virtue of its large membership, and evidence from the Sunlight Foundation found that it spent $15.1 million in 2011 successfully supporting the retention of Obama's Patient Protection and Affordable Care Act **d**. Pressure groups are useful to political parties as they aggregate views of specific groups — the two main parties are catch-all parties and this means that they use pressure groups as sources of information for what different groups want. However small groups that represent minorities have historically had success also **e** — *Brown* v *Board of Education* (1954) was funded by the NAACP and resulted in segregation being ruled illegal **f**. More recently the ACLU, which is only relatively small with half a million members, overturned DOMA in the Supreme Court case of *US* v *Windsor*, which effectively banned any federal discrimination against minority gay and lesbian couples **g**. Though these groups may have had relatively less support than larger groups, groups can still achieve their goals due to the fact that there are many ways to influence US politics — in these cases the NAACP and ACLU were able to influence the Supreme Court ruling, though pressure groups can also try to achieve their goals through Congress or at a local level through state legislatures. In short, though size is a crucial factor in achieving pressure group goals, there still remains a variety of different access points meaning that smaller groups are still able to achieve their goals **h**.

(e) The second paragraph starts well by setting out evidence that size is still an important factor to pressure group success, using **d** a good example of their influence, even if this figure is the total amount the AARP spent on lobbying in 2011 rather than directly supporting Obamacare. It continues **e** by setting out a key method of influence, through litigation, used by smaller pressure groups within the US political system. This is well supported by two relevant examples of pressure group success in this area, although **f** the first of which is far less contemporary and detailed than **g** the second. Furthermore, **h** the student is quick to analyse and clarify their judgement at the end of the paragraph showing they are remaining well focused on the question set.

Membership size has been seen to be important, particularly as often it translates into having a higher level of funding. The NRA was able to influence the gun regulation vote in the Senate (April 2013) — it provided funds to 42 out of 45 senators who opposed the bill **i**. This shows how large groups by virtue of their size can be more influential as they have more funds from membership fees. However, money is not always proportional to size — groups may be influential even though they do not represent a large base of support. Certain groups are able to be more successful as they are able to buy political influence, particularly those that are able to afford lobbyists **j**. The amount of money in US politics means that it is hard for groups with low levels of funding to be heard — this was particularly the case in the debates over healthcare from 2009. In 2012 the American Medical Association spent $16.5 million on lobbying and in the 2012 election $3.3 billion was spent by lobbying firms **k**. This shows how much money is now involved in US politics meaning that groups that are not able to spend are less likely to get their perspectives heard. There have been attempts in recent years to make money less of a contributing factor to pressure group success — this has been shown by the extension of campaign finance under FEC 1972 and 1974 and BCRA in 2002. However, the provisions of these restrictions were deconstructed through the *Buckley* v *Valeo* (1976) and *Citizens United* v *FEC* (2010) **l**. This means that pressure groups with high levels of funds are still able to influence the outcome of elections (such as by funding adverts). This was seen by the effect of Super PACs, such as 'Restore our Future', on the outcome of the 2012 election. So in short high levels of membership may mean that groups are in a better position to lobby decision makers but some groups are in a position where they can simply achieve their goals due to their level of funds, such as the way that the tobacco industry is able to outspend the health industry in terms of lobbying **m**.

(e) The student continues to evaluate the influence of different factors on pressure group success by looking at how funding is related to size with a detailed, contemporary and relevant example of **i** the NRA influence in blocking the most recent attempts at introducing gun control legislation. Similarly, the student makes a good evaluative point **j** about the importance of funding, which they separate from the size of the groups. Again **k** they support this point with a range of detailed and relevant examples. The student again shows some strong knowledge and understanding, this time of **l** the legislation and Supreme Court decisions which have affected pressure group funding, but much of this is descriptive. The student does not include a detailed example of how this has enabled a specific pressure group to influence or shape legislation successfully. The reference **m** to the success of the tobacco industry is not well supported with no particular example of how its outspending has led it to be more successful than the health industry.

> Another factor which is important to the success of groups is how close ties with political departments are — sometimes iron triangles can arise which result in certain groups being influential due to close bonds with the executive department and the Congressional committees **n**. An example of this is shown by the way defence contractors providing C-17 transporter planes were able to block attempts to reduce spending in the 2010 Defence Authorization Bill, as the Pentagon wished to keep its spending on defence high and the defence committees wished to keep jobs in the defence industry. This shows how deals can be made that are effectively elitist — regardless of the support base, other groups were not involved in these deals. There have been attempts to restrict the level to which this occurs in US politics, such as through the Open Government and Honest Leadership Act (2007), which reduced the revolving door syndrome of politicians going on to become lobbyists straight after leaving office **o**. However, it is still arguable that elitism means that some groups are more successful due to their connections, regardless of the size of their support base.

(e) The fourth paragraph examines the impact of insider status on pressure group success. It starts with a clear explanation **n** of the iron triangle, which is well supported with a detailed example. In addition to **o** the strong knowledge of the restrictions on pressure group activity the final sentence focuses back on the question, by addressing how these close ties with government can enable pressure groups to succeed regardless of their size.

> Another factor that is arguably important to the success of a pressure group is the area that it supports and how important these areas are to the two main parties **p**. AIPAC (the group representing Israel's interest in America) is a very important group as America's political relationship with Israel is very important to its foreign policy. Clearly AIPAC is in a position to influence both the Democrats and Republicans as both parties prioritise this issue — both Obama and all the main Republican contenders in 2012 spoke at AIPAC in the run up to the election. So group success is improved if the area the group is involved in is of political importance to both parties. However, this is not to say that groups cannot gain popularity over time. Groups representing women's rights have grown in political influence over the Democrat party since the 1970s and as a result these groups were able to influence the creation of the Lilly Ledbetter Act which secured equal pay for women with their male counterparts **q**. This shows that groups that represent issues that become of importance to parties over time are also likely to have success in achieving their goals.

ⓔ Here the argument is less strong, and the points made about pressure group success being related to **p** fluctuations in party policies and positions are less convincing than previous arguments. Although the reference to AIPAC is relevant and well enough supported, the latter point about **q** the rise of women's rights is quite vague, and mistakenly claims the Lilly Ledbetter Act gave equal pay rather than it allowing more time for female staff members to challenge unequal pay in the courts.

> In conclusion membership size is an important factor in pressure group success, but there are other factors which also influence this such as funds and how sympathetic their cause is to the government **r**. With increased regulation it is hoped that pressure groups will be able to compete on the basis of democratic merit rather than by distorting factors **s**.

ⓔ The conclusion **r** draws together the main factors which account for pressure group success, but does not clearly arrive at a judgement about which is the most significant factor. It ends **s** with an irrelevant reflection on how pressure group activity could be more democratic given increased regulation. Overall this is a strong answer which, despite the fact that it is less strong in places, would achieve an A grade in the exam.

AO1 KNOWLEDGE AND UNDERSTANDING: Throughout the answer the student uses a very good and broad range of examples, most of which are relevant to the question set and are well developed. In this way **g** the example in the second paragraph, on the successful use of litigation, not only mentions the size of the ACLU (half a million members) but also details the act which it challenged (DOMA) and the specific case which was brought to the Supreme Court (*US v Windsor*).

AO2 EVALUATION AND ANALYSIS: In places there are very good evaluative comments and most of the essay is analytical with the student looking to explore a range of factors which contribute to pressure group success. In places however this is less strong and the student does not fully weigh up competing arguments to support a clear judgement, on which is the most important factor, as best highlighted by their **r** weak conclusion.

SYNOPTICITY: This essay does deal with a range of competing arguments about the different factors which affect pressure group success. Overall it provides evidence to support at least two views on the question despite the fact that it is sometimes drawn into a discussion of the irrelevant debate about the democratic nature of pressure group activity.

AO3 COMMUNICATION: The essay flows well, although some of the points are not well connected and it does not fully present an argument on which is the most important factor.

ⓔ **36/45 marks awarded:** 11/12 for AO1, 9/12 for AO2, 9/12 for synopticity, 7/9 for AO3.

It is usually easy to get an idea about how successful a pressure group is — it comes down to how prevalent the group is in the public eye, how it impacts elections and politicians, and most importantly, how it affects legislation **a**. There is also a lot of controversy with this as some argue that pressure groups are elitist, and damage democracy. This is because only a few pressure groups tend to hold power and have a lot of influence over the US political system. However others argue that they are good for democracy and believe that competition between pressure groups in a pluralist democracy is healthy for the US political system **b**. However, it is clear that many different things contribute to pressure group success **c**, even if some people think this is a good or bad thing.

ⓔ This introduction seems to start well with **a** a good focus on setting down some criteria for the measurement of pressure group success. However, it soon draws away from the question **b** by looking at whether pressure group activity is a healthy part of the US political system. Although this could be made relevant, perhaps by linking the elitist argument to the factors which allow a small number of pressure groups to dominate the political system, no real credit is given for this point as the student does little to relate this wider elitist and pluralist debate to the question set. Although this answer does come back to the question at the end of this introduction **c** this is very generalised and fails to signpost specific factors which affect pressure group success.

On one hand, there are many examples of pressure groups achieving great success on issues based on large membership. The AARP is the biggest pressure group in the USA with millions of retired members, and it has used this to achieve notable successes in getting better government services for its older members **d**. This includes pressuring George Bush to get cheaper drugs **e**. However another factor for success is using the Supreme Court to get favourable decisions **f**. The NAACP and the ACLU have won progressive court cases such as the landmark ruling on 1954 *Brown* v *Board of Education of Topeka*, which proved very successful. Civil rights became almost a defining issue of the late 1950s and early 1960s and black people were finally universally given the vote in 1965. Although the civil rights movement was a populist one, often perceived as a triumph that came only from the sheer numbers and desperation of its activists and supporters their success came from the Supreme Court, not their size **g**. Arguably, trade union pressure groups, such as the AFL-CIO, proved instrumental in the fight for labour rights in the early part of the twentieth century, although much was due to striking as a tactic, which is somewhat unique to trade unions **h**.

ⓔ The second paragraph is more directly focused on the question, with a better understanding of a large pressure group **d**, and what appears to be a limited attempt **e** to show its influence on the passage of the 2003 Medicare, Prescription Drug Act. However, it then stumbles into an evaluation of a further factor for success, namely **f** the use of litigation through the Supreme Court. Although this does not flow well from the previous point the student is addressing the question more directly with a relevant, if rather typical, example of the success of the NAACP. **g** The evaluation of this factor on their success is better expressed at the end of the paragraph even though the student fails to give a specific example of how the ACLU achieved similar success through the Supreme Court. Similarly, the final point **h** about the success of the AFL-CIO, though a relevant pressure group, is not well made or supported and it does not flow from the previous discussion.

However, on the other hand, when it comes to money versus size, money has often won out. While the NRA is often cited for its high membership (3 million strong... and they vote) contributing to its success at congressional level, this is more due to its Victory Fund **i**. This effectively nullified the Brady Bill and killed the most recent attempts at gun control **j**. This is arguably only the case because of the high levels of funding the NRA receives from gun manufacturers — wealthy businesses that obviously have a vested interest in the success of the NRA.

e The third paragraph does well to elaborate on the argument that funds are more important than size, with reference to **i** the NRA and its financial war chest. Again however it lacks detail on **j** the examples used, such as how the Brady Bill was 'nullified' by the concessions achieved during its passage through Congress and the subsequent *Printz* v *US* decision. The student also fails to explain fully how the NRA had funded all but three senators who voted against the measures for closer background checks in April 2013.

Historically iron triangles have also proved instrumental in the success of elitist pressure groups **k**, that is to say, K-Street lobbying firms acting on behalf of big business, something which President Eisenhower touched upon when he warned against the powerful Military Industrial Complex in his final speech as president. A famous example is the iron triangle with weapons producers during the Iraq War — they used their contacts on congressional committees and in the Pentagon to secure higher spending on military contracts that benefited them all **l**. This relates to the 'revolving-door syndrome', where senators and congressmen leave their jobs and work for K-Street lobbying firms, getting high-paid lobbying jobs 2 years after they leave Congress **m**. It is this insider status which guarantees success, rather than the size of a pressure group. This is seen with small insider groups like the Jewish lobby groups having more impact on legislation and getting favourable decisions for Israel, despite them only being small in size **n**.

e In this paragraph the student continues to present the disconnected factors which account for pressure group success, by referring to the importance of gaining insider status. Initially they mention the importance of **k** iron triangles showing some knowledge of this, even if **l** the example is once again very broad and lacks the detail expected for a stronger response. The paragraph continues by referring to a further related point **m** on the influence of the revolving door, and by alluding to the power of **n** the 'Jewish lobby'. This presents a solid case for the importance of insider status to pressure group success but could have been much improved if the student had referred specifically to AIPAC and used specific examples to show how it has successfully shaped US foreign policy due to its insider status.

In conclusion, while size can be an important factor in determining pressure group success, the most important factor is money **o**. Most pressure group successes have come from lobbying firms representing the interests of big business and wealthy investors (especially those able to fund election campaigns by setting up Super PACs **p**). While some examples exist of populist pressure group activity or those who use the Supreme Court achieving success most success comes from those groups which have the most money **q**.

(e) The conclusion does focus on the question, and reiterates **o** the student's viewpoint that the most important factor for pressure group success is 'money'. Indeed they assert that this is the crucial factor and introduce the importance of **p** funding 'election campaigns' through the use of Super PACs. However, they have not developed this in the main body and have instead introduced it at the end without specific examples of how campaign funding has helped achieve electoral success for certain pressure groups. Despite this they clearly set out **q** their concluding argument that money is the key to pressure group success. Overall, this student shows a solid level of knowledge, despite the patchy nature of the argument presented. The answer as a whole would achieve a C grade in the exam.

AO1 KNOWLEDGE AND UNDERSTANDING: There are some good passages of knowledge though most of it lacks specific detail. Most points have a degree of explanation, which shows a sound understanding of the essay question. The student is also credited for their broad spread of knowledgeable points, especially those relating to **d** size, **f** litigation, **i** funding and **k** insider status.

AO2 EVALUATION AND ANALYSIS: The student evaluates a range of factors which account for pressure group success, but sometimes the analysis and evaluation is disjointed. In this way points **f** and **h** do not flow well from the preceding ones which somewhat detracts from the AO2 marks. The lack of a balanced argument restricts the student's ability to show a higher level of evaluation, which depresses the overall mark in this area. Similarly, this response explains a range of factors but fails to evaluate fully and convincingly to support its argument that funding is the crucial factor to pressure group success.

SYNOPTICITY: There is a clear balance to this essay, which seems to weigh up at least four factors (**d** size, **f** litigation, **i** funding and **k** insider status). Although some of these are less well developed there is a clear sense that the student is aware of the competing synoptic debate on the question.

AO3 COMMUNICATION: The answer flows well enough, if it is a bit disjointed in places, and has a solid structure which make a series of clear points relevant to the question.

(e) **27/45 marks awarded:** 8/12 for AO1, 6/12 for AO2, 7/12 for synopticity, 6/9 for AO3.

Question 4 Racial and ethnic politics

To what extent is it true that equality remains a distant dream for most minority groups in the USA?

ⓔ This question is asking whether or not minority groups, which would include African Americans, Latinos and Asians, have achieved true equality in America today. The use of the term 'To what extent' points towards the need for an evaluation of the evidence about *both* the political, social and economic opportunities for American minorities, *and* the evidence that they lack opportunities in these areas. Higher-level responses should be able to recognise and differentiate between the different experiences of equality among different ethnic and racial groups, rather than considering 'minority groups' as a cohesive body.

Student A

After the Supreme Court ruling of *Brown* v *Board of Education* the Supreme Court justices ruled the constitution to be 'colour blind', abolishing the Jim Crow laws and finally making the constitution support equality. Affirmative action was introduced to help ethnic minorities where they had in the past been overlooked **a**. However, the liberal argument remains that America is far from achieving racial equality **b**.

ⓔ Although this is a solid introduction, which **a** sets out the historical context and **b** relates this to the views of liberals, it could be improved by more clearly signposting the wider contemporary debate surrounding the question of equality, to secure synoptic marks.

In terms of political representation, ethnic minorities are relatively well represented in the House **c**. Although its make-up is not proportional to the different races in the country, racial equality in the House has come on a long way, with the 113th Congress including 41 African-American representatives, such as Georgia's Hank Johnson, and 34 Latino representatives, such as Illinois' Luis Gutierrez **d**. Similarly, the Supreme Court can be seen as a melting pot of cultures, with newly-elected Latino Justice Sonia Sotomayor and African-American Justice Clarence Thomas **e**. The Senate, however, shows minorities, especially African Americans, to be very poorly represented with only two African Americans securing victory in the 2012 election **f**. Although there is a better level of ethnic minority representation in the House, this does not necessarily show equality in America — many of these representatives come from especially created majority-minority districts such as Illinois' 4th district represented by Luis Guitierez or Maryland's 3rd district, which was recently referred to as a 'crazy quilt' in the *Washington Post*. While those majority-minority districts do make the House more representative, the fact that voting districts have to be gerrymandered to enable ethnic minorities to get in to these positions suggests equality is still a distant dream **g**.

ⓔ The student uses the second paragraph to **c** evaluate the issue of political equality. They make excellent use of a wide range of very detailed examples to support their argument about the level of equality suggested by the level of political representation, among both African Americans and Latinos. Indeed they give a spread of examples, showing good depth of knowledge, from **d** the House, **e** the Supreme Court and **f** the Senate. The student uses the Senate example well to temper their judgement and set out the areas of ongoing inequality, as best evidenced by their concluding sentence **g** that the need for majority-minority districts suggests that the USA is still not fully equal.

Much better representation is seen at state level with a number of predominantly white areas having African-American state legislatures. Jerry Green, for example, is an African-American state legislature in the 22nd district of New Jersey where nearly 60% of the population is white. Similarly, in Colorado, African Americans make up less than 4% of the population yet in 2009 the House and Senate were led by two African Americans: Terence Carroll and Peter Groff **h**. The fact that ethnic minorities can win elections in these predominantly white areas suggests racial equality is much closer than some liberals believe, especially when one considers how supportive Colorado was of Jim Crow laws and slavery **i**.

🅔 Again the student shows excellent depth of knowledge in **h** evaluating political representation at a state level, with a range of comprehensive examples. **i** This is well rounded up at the end of the paragraph, which links to the student's line of argument that there is more equality than some liberals might suggest.

In terms of social and economic equality, figures clearly show that both African Americans and Latinos earn less, and are less likely to graduate college **j**. African Americans are on average more likely to go to prison than white people, and as a result of this nearly 13% of blacks cannot vote. However, other ethnic minorities such as Asians now almost match whites on employment, education and wage statistics, suggesting that the American political system is not, as some liberals would say, intrinsically racist. Indeed in a book 'no excuses' it claims that African Americans are further behind whites because of cultural issues **k**.

🅔 This paragraph deals with the other criteria for measuring equality, namely social and economic, less well. It starts by summarising the problems faced, with **j** relevant but not particularly detailed examples. Similarly, though the student evaluates this by reviewing alternative evidence, this lacks the depth of knowledge shown earlier. Indeed the student could develop **k** the points, which effectively refer to model minorities, by specifying the evidence to support exactly how 'African Americans are further behind whites', such as the findings in a 2013 report by the Institute on Assets and Social Policy which found evidence that the wealth gap between white and African Americans tripled between 1984 and 2009.

The view favoured by many conservatives, including African-American Supreme Court Justice Clarence Thomas, is that ethnic minorities should make no excuses. They argue that for genuine racial equality America must be a truly colour-blind society, meaning outlawing, as Arizona did in its 2010 midterm proposition **l**, affirmative action. For many, affirmative action is little more than 'positive racism', which, far from helping ethnic minorities, disadvantages them, making them lazy. This view is disputed by groups like the NAACP who push for more affirmative action believing it is the only way to ensure racial equality **m**.

e The fifth paragraph is also not as strong because it could be more clearly related to the question. Though it **l** sets out the conservative argument regarding equality, this drifts into the views of affirmative action. **m** The ending should look to explicitly link the points made earlier to the question set, and the student's judgement on how far this would suggest that equality was a 'distant dream'.

> With America being a federal country it is difficult to say whether the country as a whole has equality or not. Many expect the 'liberal north' to be colour blind while the 'conservative south' is expected to still hold racist views, but this view is disputed by figures. For example a 2005 report from the Council of State governments found that between 1981 and 2005 African-American state representatives doubled, while Latinos trebled. Similarly a 2012 report showed that many southern states, such as Mississippi which is nearly 60% white, have representation ranging from 20 to 23%. This shows the increasing representation of ethnic minorities, particularly in states which throughout the 1960s were regarded as racist **n**.
>
> Overall it is clear that while America is not yet a country with complete equality, shown through the lack of African-American representation in the Senate, it has come a long way to achieving racial equality, with Barack Obama, an African American, holding the most powerful job in the country as president.

e The two final paragraphs show the strengths of this answer, which is an excellent attempt to engage with and evaluate the question set. The student's ability to **n** weigh up and evaluate evidence is shown at the end of the penultimate paragraph, where it explains what the evidence of state-level representation suggests about equality. The conclusion summarises the line of argument throughout. In an exam this very strong answer would achieve an A grade.

AO1 KNOWLEDGE AND UNDERSTANDING: An excellent range of examples shows substantial depth of knowledge on the level of political representation (especially points **d**, **e**, **f** & **h**). A more detailed understanding of the evidence surrounding social and economic equality (**j** & **k**) would secure an even higher mark in this area.

AO2 EVALUATION AND ANALYSIS: Although there is a very good level of evaluation regarding the issue of political equality throughout, the failure to fully develop an analysis of wider measures of equality somewhat limits the mark in this area.

SYNOPTICITY: This answer shows a good understanding of different interpretations on the question. However, further reference to the contemporary debate, such as in **b** the opening paragraph, and more explicit linkages to the question of (**l**) the conservative views shown in the fifth paragraph, could raise the synoptic marks further.

AO3 COMMUNICATION: Overall this is a very well-structured response, which fluently sets out the key points in separate paragraphs. The argument is well balanced but flows easily throughout the essay.

38/45 marks awarded: 10/12 for AO1, 9/12 for AO2, 10/12 for synopticity, 9/9 for AO3.

Student B

The USA was founded upon principles of freedom, liberty and equality, and until this day is recognised as the land of opportunity. However, fundamentally the constitution has undermined minority equality throughout history and particularly minority groups, such as Native Americans, still are perceived as 'second-class' citizens **a**. Initially, when the constitution was created, Article 1, section 2, clause 3 'excluded Indians' and classed African Americans as 'three fifths' of a person, thus creating a society in which equality is acceptable to only the 'majority' **b**.

Many conservatives would argue the last presidential election shows this dream, for black Americans, has been realised **c**. 2008 saw the election of Barack Obama, the first black president ever. Before this election in national government they would argue the presence of African Americans in positions of power shows equality of opportunity. Colin Powell and Condoleezza Rice are examples of this. Furthermore in the Supreme Court the emergence of the black Clarence Thomas adds to this argument **d**.

🅮 The introduction **a** sets down the historical context to the question well and also relates this to the contemporary synoptic debate among **b** liberals, that equality is largely the preserve of the 'majority', and **c** conservatives, that political representation shows that the dream has been realised for all Americans. Although the student supports this second point well with relevant examples to show a degree of political representation, **d** these examples are somewhat broad, and certainly in the case of Powell and Rice quite dated. The student could easily have improved this by replacing these examples with more recent and detailed examples, such as those presented by Student A.

Despite claims from conservative supporters of theories such as 'no excuses' that racism no longer exists, many minorities view equality as a distant dream **e**.

🅮 The student here makes a short but relevant point, which summarises the alternative argument and links well into the next paragraph. However, the point is not developed, with **e** no detail given on which conservative authors have proclaimed racism no longer exists or the basis for views that equality is a distant dream.

Within political institutions, minority groups are extremely under-represented, demonstrated through there being only two African Americans in the Senate currently, despite comprising 13% of the population **f**. However, conservatives point towards figures such as President Obama, Justice Clarence Thomas and Colorado's state president, who had positions of great power, to demonstrate that freedom of opportunity does exist **g**. Yet moderate liberals call for equality of outcome, as Bill Clinton famously described he wanted a cabinet which 'looked like America', only then shall equality be achieved. In contrast, in positions of power and responsibility, candidates cannot be appointed merely for equal representation, rather equality should not compromise ability and qualification **h**.

🅮 This paragraph opens well, with **f** a relevant example regarding under-representation in the Senate. Again, however, the extent and accuracy of this knowledge is shown to be less thorough by the later examples, given that **g** the first two of these are repeated from the second paragraph, while the third is wrong, probably referring to the fact that in 2008 both the State legislative chambers for

Colorado were led by African Americans. Similarly, towards the end of this paragraph, the student **h** drifts from the question and makes quite a confused and poorly explained point regarding Clinton's administration and what appears to be a personal judgement not really related to the question.

> Since the civil rights movements in the 1960s and Supreme Court decisions such as *Brown* v *Board of Education* (1954), segregationist educational systems were illegal and methods such as bussing and quotas have been introduced as an attempt to create equality within education **i**. However, equality of outcome has not been achieved, with drop-out rates extremely high among Latino communities and minorities' lower representation in higher education. Moderate and pragmatic conservatives point towards the growing rate of African Americans graduating from high school, with currently 89% compared to 36% in the 1970s **j**.

e The fifth paragraph does not flow well from the preceding one and **i** merely sets out the historical context of the liberal argument, without initially making an analytical point. It does then draw back into the question with **j** a well-developed look at areas of ongoing educational inequality.

> This demonstrates that equality is slowly being achieved **k** and conservatives point towards the findings of 'no excuses' and achievements of model minorities such as Asians, whose graduation and average income exceeded those of whites in 2004, to indicate both the possibility of equality of outcome, which are no longer limited by social and inherent problems **l**.

e The concluding paragraph continues the student's argument that **k** there is general equality in the USA. **l** Again it points towards outline evidence for this among the Asian community, without presenting any specific or detailed evidence to reinforce the judgement. In fact the essay comes to an abrupt end and the student does not appear to have fully summarised the extent to which they agree with the question or the basis for that judgement. Overall this essay is a sound answer. It has some irrelevance, but largely focuses on the question, and would manage to get a C grade in the exam.

AO1 KNOWLEDGE AND UNDERSTANDING: Although there is some sound knowledge in places (such as points **d**, **f** & **j**), on the whole the knowledge is quite basic, with some points either lacking full development (as with **d**, **e** & **l**) or others being wrong or irrelevant (**g** & **h**).

AO2 EVALUATION AND ANALYSIS: The answer does attempt to address the question and present a balanced argument. However, the line of argument is not entirely clear while at times **h** it drifts away from the question.

SYNOPTICITY: Solid understanding of at least two views on the question, namely the liberal and conservative debate over the degree of equality, is shown.

AO3 COMMUNICATION: Although on the whole there is some structure to the answer, **i** the extent to which this flows throughout is limited. Similarly, the lack of a clear conclusion contributes to the loss of marks in this area.

23/45 marks awarded: 6/12 for AO1, 6/12 for AO2, 7/12 for synopticity, 4/9 for AO3.

Knowledge check answers

1 US system of government which divides power between the national (federal) government and the local (state) government, each having separate lawmaking powers.

2 An electoral system in which the winner only needs to achieve a simple majority of the vote to win (one more vote than the nearest opponent). It is a winner-takes-all system, in that nothing is allocated to runners-up, unlike more proportional systems.

3 Iowa is the first state to vote in the presidential nominating process, while New Hampshire holds the first primary. As a result, both the Iowa caucus and the New Hampshire primary receive huge amounts of attention from presidential nominees, as well as media coverage. Good or bad showings in these early elections can therefore make or break a candidate.

4 Pledged delegates are committed to vote for a certain candidate in the first ballot of votes. Superdelegates are leading party figures who have not been committed to vote for a candidate in the primary process.

5 Every 2 years all members of the House (2-year terms) and one-third of the Senate (6-year terms) face re-election. The president is elected every 4 years.

6 The congressional elections which take place midway through a president's term of office. During this time the entire House and one-third of the Senate face re-election.

7 Factions could include the Tuesday Group, Main Street Republicans, the Tea Party Caucus or the Religious Right.

8 For the Republican Party, these could include the Tea Party Caucus; the Republican Tuesday Group; the Main Street Partnership. For the Democrats, groups would include the Congressional Progressive Caucus; the New Democrat Coalition; the Blue Dog Coalition.

9 Pro-life views oppose abortion on moral grounds and advocate a legal ban. In contrast, pro-choice views advance a woman's legal right to terminate a pregnancy.

10 The institution established by the Founding Fathers to indirectly elect the president of the USA. Each state is given a certain number of electors, equal to the number of senators and representatives. A candidate must receive over 270 Electoral College votes to secure the presidency.

11 The US political system separates the three main branches of government: the executive (President); the legislature (Congress); and the judiciary (Supreme Court). In addition to this, the powers of each branch overlap so that they hold each other to account, or check and balance each other.

12 These are elections, which take place before a general election, to choose a party's candidate for that election. In these primaries party supporters usually vote in order to choose the party's candidate for political office.

13 Under the FECA 1974, individual contributions to a candidate were limited to $1,000. Under the BCRA 2002, the amount was raised to $2,000, but would increase with inflation.

14 'Hard money' refers to those contributions given directly to a candidate or their campaign team. 'Soft money' refers to those unregulated funds given to national political parties, or unregulated independent organisations which are not directly linked to candidate campaigns, such as 527s.

15 Methods include collecting signatures to introduce a ballot initiative, and coordinating, funding or staffing a specific campaign.

16 As well as the Senate being one chamber of the legislature, meaning it is targeted because of its lawmaking role, it is also a target because of its foreign policy powers, its role in confirming appointments and the individual senator's filibuster powers.

17 *Lawrence* v *Texas* effectively safeguarded an individual's right to a same-sex relationship while the *Windsor* v *US* ruling declared the Defence of Marriage Act unconstitutional, as it allowed the federal government to discriminate against same-sex marriages.

18 Lobbying is the process whereby pressure groups aim to influence policy makers, which are usually lawmakers, through persuasion and the information they provide to those who need it.

19 The pressure group which funded *Brown* v *Board of Education* was the National Association for the Advancement of Colored People (NAACP).

20 Post-racial America is the view that race is no longer an issue in the USA. The political, economic and social achievements of minorities have been used as evidence that race is no longer a barrier to success.

21 Conservatives believe in equality of opportunity, which is guaranteed by ensuring all races and ethnic groups are free from discrimination, and thus have the same chances as whites. Liberals, however, believe in equality of outcome and would point to the existence of lingering institutional racism which, despite legal protection against racism and discrimination, results in ongoing disadvantages for minority groups.

22 Restrictions in affirmative action have come through Supreme Court decisions which have limited the scope of its programmes and through a series of initiatives and propositions which have banned its use across some states.

23 In 2003 the *Gratz* v *Bollinger* case declared the University of Michigan's racial quota system of admissions unconstitutional as it was 'too mechanistic'. In contrast, the *Grutter* v *Bollinger* case upheld the UCLA's Law School admissions policy, with its more 'individualised' approach to affirmative action.